Advance Praise for
Potential

"Individuals and organizations in the social profit sector are always looking to elevate our impact in pursuit of the mission. *Potential* provides insightful ideas and approaches that can enable each of us to find new energy and power within ourselves and our teams by capitalizing on the potential that already exists. This book is a thoughtful resource that can strengthen individuals, teams, and organizations to deliver next-level impact."
—Meaghan Stovel McKnight, CEO, Make-A-Wish Canada

"I have had the pleasure of collaborating with Pam over the last decade with my Northland Properties and WestJet teams. Pam's authentic approach and deep expertise in leadership development truly resonated with us. She has a remarkable talent for simplifying complex ideas and fostering a culture of meaningful engagement and growth. Her guidance was instrumental in helping us uncover and embrace our core values and mission, leading to more cohesive and purpose-driven organizations."
—Manoj Jasra, CMO & SVP, Strategy @Accolite

"Her direct yet warm style engages, challenges, and supports others in their development journey—whether verbally or in writing. She succeeds in making the complex understandable and actionable."
—Jocelyn Bérard, Author, International Talent Management Expert

"There is no one like the dynamic Pam August! Our team leaves every interaction with her inspired, motivated, and ready to act. Thank you, Pam, for helping us set the stage for unprecedented collaboration and success. Lavender would not be where we are today without you!"
—Pritma Dhillon-Chattha and Brighid Gannon, Cofounders, Lavender

"So many of my career and life lessons are rooted in my work with Pam. She has a way of developing the people around her beyond a 'presentation' or a 'neat idea.' She has the rare ability to inspire people to be different and sustain different. Not many practitioners in the learning and development or culture space have had a sustained positive impact on my abilities as a leader, practitioner, parent, and spouse. This book brings her impact together in one place, all the ingredients she has learned, shared, and used with leaders across Canada. It brings her powerful learning to life in ways that are as unique as she is in the talent development space. Not just talent development—being a better all-around human."

—MONICA MOCHORUK, Vice President, Talent Management, Parkland Corporation

"Pam's impact is life-changing and I should know. Not only did she help with my homework growing up, she DID IT! Years and hundreds of awards, including three Emmys (and numerous more nominations) later, I count Pam as the best sister someone could have and the best guide and support through the challenges of work and life. While she calls herself the 'underachiever in the family,' after reading *Potential*, I know you will agree that she is also far too humble."

—JEFF AUGUST, Partner, Creative Director, Jump Studios

"Our Rümi team had the absolute pleasure of partnering with Pam at the onset of our culture journey, which included leaning on her expertise to listen and learn from our people, cocreate our values, and develop engaging, unique culture activations aligned with our brand purpose. Pam's amazing ability to connect with our diverse employee population and bring out their potential was instrumental in building our successful culture foundation and continued business results!"

—NICOLE MURRAY, Champion, Employee Experience & Culture at Rümi, Powered by ATCO

"Pam does magic with teams. I don't know how she does it, but she manages to transform and innovate groups that are stale in thinking, resistant to change, obstinate to innovation, and hate new things."
—Tomas Nilsson, Executive Director Strategic Data, Analytics and Business Services

"Pam August helped me better understand my actions as a mother, partner, leader, and professional. I now tap into my North Star as a leader by looking within to bring my energy and strengths, helping me to listen better and hear myself, powerfully guiding my practice and successes. I appreciate how our conversations have allowed me to see how I can convert my unique potential into impact and feel authentic in how I relate to the complexity of our worlds! I sincerely enjoy the time I spend with Pam, and I am sure you will too. Think of *Potential* like having Pam as your coach in a written form."
—Raynie Wood, PhD, Dean, SAIT School for Advanced Digital Technology

"*Potential* is a powerful book by a powerful author. Pam August's voice resonates throughout as she teaches you how to remove whatever is in your way, get unstuck, and 'connect the potential' that she argues lies within each and every one of us. Reading her words is akin to working with Pam herself, and doing so is a blessing for anyone striving to realize their best."
—Ashley Mansour, International Bestselling Author, Founder of LA Writing Coach and Brands Through Books

"I've worked with Pam for over fourteen years. She knows her subject matter incredibly well after leading culture strategy for one of the most successful brands in Canadian history. She has taken what she was passionate about as a leader—learning, growing, and connecting people with purpose in her role at WestJet—to her consulting, speaking, and writing. Her enthusiasm and passion for people shines through in her

words and actions. She offers truly unique ideas and insights that are intentional and impactful. All with thoughtful spirit and levity."
—MARNIE BALLANE, Senior Vice President, Speakers Spotlight

"During our time together at WestJet, Pam brought unique insight and inspiration to the development of our culture and all WestJetters who contributed to its evolution. She challenged and broadened the thinking of the organization's leadership and worked with me to ignite the ownership mindset of all fourteen thousand employees. Working with Pam is both effective and energizing. *Potential* is the next best thing to having the opportunity to work directly with her."
—GREGG SARETSKY, Board Chair, Former CEO and President, WestJet

"Pam is a wizard with words and a unique ability to make them click and stick. And not just stick but translate powerfully to action that is life-altering. *'You can't nutrition yourself into good health'* set the foundation for my business and offering into the world—reframing it from nutrition to nourish. When you read *Potential,* it will feel like Pam is right there with you, and even though she isn't physically there, her masterful way of helping others notice the potential within themselves will allow you to see yours."
—JAMEY KAY, Founder, With Love From Jamey

POTENTIAL

POTENTIAL

How to Connect
What's Already There for
Exponential Impact

PAM AUGUST

Post Hill
PRESS

A POST HILL PRESS BOOK
ISBN: 979-8-88845-417-6
ISBN (eBook): 979-8-88845-418-3

Potential:
How to Connect What's Already There for Exponential Impact
© 2024 by Pam August
All Rights Reserved

Cover design by Jim Villaflores

Post Hill Press
New York • Nashville
posthillpress.com

Published in the United States of America
1 2 3 4 5 6 7 8 9 10

To everyone I have ever learned and connected potential with.
Because you are reading this, everyone includes you.

TABLE OF CONTENTS

Deep Problems Evoke Deep Potential

T his is the story of a twentysomething college student. A student who was always told that they had so much potential if only they would just "apply" themselves. Despite the fact that they were passionate about learning and desperately trying their best, their potential was not fully realized. True, they were encouraged at an early age—like by their fourth-grade teacher, Miss O'Sullivan, who wrote that they "added the spice that every classroom needed." But still, the stories of what they were missing were the ones that played most often in their head, creating an inner world of pressure and an outer world of expectation. When they started college, studying health and nutrition, the student thought that they had finally found "it"—a learning path and career that they were passionate about and willing to fully apply themselves to—and they dove in.

Early in the program, they found themselves being targeted and picked on by an instructor who was also the head of the program with decision-making power about the future of all students in their important second-year workplace learning placements. The student didn't know this at the time, but this instructor had a pattern of having one "scapegoat" each year, usually a student who showed high potential but needed to be "put in their place" and kept in line. This role was unofficial—not explicitly spoken about but implicitly known by the "victim" and those around them. This year, this student was it.

Despite the digs, belittlement, and obstacles by this instructor along the way, they persevered, even stepping up to help other students who were also struggling in this toxic learning environment. They were proud of how they were applying themselves and the steps they were taking toward their potential. Still, things came to a head six weeks before the end of the program's first year, when students received confirmation of where they were being placed for the next twelve months of their workplace learning experience. This was a pivotal part of the program, because where students were placed impacted their career success post-graduation. The student in this story had already been awarded a prestigious assignment for nine months of the workplace learning year because of their academic performance, but they volunteered to take a less desirable location for the remaining three months to give more opportunity to other students. Their offer was dismissed by the program head with a reminder to "let them run the program."

On the second last day of the first year, in front of the whole class, the instructor announced a last-minute change in placements that meant this student now needed to move out of the city to start their workplace learning in just three weeks. This last-minute change meant that they had to break their apartment lease, find a new place to live, quit their part-time job, and find part-time employment in a small town to pay for their schooling. When the student raised their hand, and asked the reason for the last-minute change, the instructor told them to stop rudely disrupting the class and meet in the program office at the end of the day.

Once in the instructor's office, which was complete with a comfortable couch and soft lighting to create a psychologically safe environment (irony noted), the instructor sat the student down and said, "I am having this conversation with you now because I care about you, and you need to know what I am about to say." They then continued, "You have a personality defect that will prevent you from ever being successful in life, and it is better you know it now rather than later." Yes, this is a direct quote—may I repeat it: You have a personality defect that will prevent you from ever being successful in life.

The student's mind went blank in that moment from the shock of those horrific words. What followed was a blurt of expletives, an explosion of tears, and them running from the room desperately seeking some support. Thankfully, support was provided by their parents, a mentor in the program, and a college administration team that was committed to making the situation right. But that is not the point of this story.

The point is this—while the student was devastated and demoralized, this terrible conversation planted a seed, and the seed was this: *I will never make anyone feel the way you have made me feel now.* This student could have crumbled and did for a time, but it didn't become a problem they carried for life. Instead, this moment of deep difficulty evoked the deep potential in them, potential that continued to connect through a life of learning and impact. You see, the learner in this story is me, and this is my story.

My heart still pounds as I recount it all these years later. I can't tell you what the "personality defect" was that my instructor saw in me because I didn't stick around to ask. In retrospect, I believe that my potential and my passion to connect it was threatening to her. As destructive as this experience was at the time, the deep difficulty brought out the deep potential in me that now many learning cycles and seasons later led to the conception of this book. I hope you agree with me throughout the book that it was worth it.

And a short sidebar to the story. In the small town that I was relocated to, I met a wonderful nurse who said I needed to meet her wonderful brother. One blind date and several wonderful years later, he is my husband and the father of our two wonderful sons—that's a lot of wonderful and some serious potential connected along the way.

WHAT'S IN THE WAY *IS* THE WAY

"What's in the way is the way" is a paraphrase from the teachings of Lao Tzu, an ancient Daoist philosopher. In this simple phrase, he not only implies that difficulties evoke potential, he commands it. I would have never imagined all those years ago that this conversation, this deeply difficult incident would be *the* catalyst for a lifetime of learning and impact that I am so happy to share with you now. It started with something I did not want. But something *in* the way soon became *the* way in ways that I could have never imagined. And while the details of this story are uniquely mine, I know that you have stories that while uniquely yours are similar in their depth of difficulty and ability to evoke your potential.

So it is not a stretch to say that I know right now there are challenging situations you are facing. And as much as you don't like it or it makes you uncomfortable, you know the truth to Lao Tzu's words: what's in the way *is* the way. Situations where you are in continuing conflict with someone who matters to you, where you just can't get traction on something important because of the roadblocks in the way, or where you are doubting yourself to make the difference you desire to make. And yet you know you need to move forward and go through it. It's like the old nursery rhyme and Michael Rosen's book of the same name, "Going on a Bear Hunt": you "can't go over it. Can't go under it. Can't go around it. Got to go through it."

It is also likely that you can recall a situation, one that felt really challenging, and see that it was this difficulty that became *the* way for you to develop, grow, and connect your potential. By going through it, you were able to build resilience—the capacity that we all have to grow stronger through challenge and adversity. For a moment, hold this book in one hand and raise your other hand if your answer is "yes" to the following questions:

- ❑ Do you admire people who are resilient? (raise your hand if yes)

- ❑ Would you like to be resilient? (keep your hand up if yes)

- ❑ Would you like to go through the difficulties, challenges, and problems necessary to develop the muscle of resilience? (I imagine your hand just went down)

The reality of resilience is that it only develops through difficulty or challenge. There is no app for it—sorry! While we can connect potential in situations that aren't difficult or challenging, what I have found is that difficulty and challenge lead to the *most* powerful connections of potential. These situations develop our resilience muscles and result in lasting transformation in their impact. I share this insight with you now before we dive into the world of connecting potential so that you don't dismiss my ideas by thinking, "That's nice in a perfect world, but my world is far from perfect." Trust me (and be encouraged) that when things are tough is when potential is most powerfully connected.

Still unsure? Let's make this idea real. Think about a time when you encountered a problem or challenge—something that was "in the way." Place yourself in that situation, much like I did in the story of the learner, and feel the experience and its impact on you. And because I am not physically there with you right now, I suggest you pick something with "medium heat" or difficulty, not something so challenging that it causes you distress at this moment.

As you reflect on this situation, ask yourself the following questions:

- What was the learning and growth that I experienced because of this difficulty? How did I become more resilient by going through it?

- What potential was connected by what was in the way? *Because* of it, not despite it.

I am confident that you have uncovered, discovered, or rediscovered something of value because you are here right now reading this book looking to grow further. So, let's jump in and unlock your next level of growth together. Welcome to *Potential: How to Connect What's Already There for Exponential Impact*!

CHAPTER ONE

Welcome to Potential: How to connect what's already there for exponential impact

THE WORLD IS A VUCA PLACE

When working with organizations to shift their cultures, I often must remind them not to expect a "big bang" change when working with human systems, because it does not exist. This assertion was proven wrong in March 2020, when the world hit "control alt delete," and our ways of working, living, and connecting (or in many cases disconnecting) changed literally overnight. The period since that moment has certainly been a "VUCA" one—volatile, uncertain, complex, and ambiguous. This acronym was first used by the US military in 1987 to describe the conditions of world conflict in the post–Cold War period. It has been adopted more broadly in the world of business accurately describing the set of conditions and challenges we find ourselves experiencing in modern life.

The problems that we face in a VUCA world are often perpetual—meaning that while we may solve or resolve the specifics in each moment, similar problems reveal themselves in the next instance, resulting in repeated eruptions of conflict, continuing confusion and uncertainty, and difficulties navigating the complexities and ambiguities of work and life. If any of this sounds familiar, don't feel alone. Marita Fridjhon, cofounder and CEO of Center for Right Relationships, teaches that these perpetual challenges are part of being a human navigating a VUCA world and they impact us all. I know that my experience in work and in life supports this claim, and I imagine that yours does as well. The impacts of navigating a VUCA world and the perpetual challenges that come with it are many. Below are three that likely at some time or another show up for us all. I call them the states of the "Three Ss"—Strain, Stuck, and Swirl. I invite you to take a moment to reflect on them now.

1. Strain—that feeling of being worn out, held back, or con-strained from what you want to achieve or the experience you want to have. Instead of feeling ease you feel tension, and moving forward feels painful. Just reading this might cause you to hold your breath, so take a moment to exhale before continuing.

2. Swirl—that feeling where you are so busy that your head wants to spin off your body. Even though there is so much going on, there is nothing getting done, leaving you exhausted and having a hard time even catching a breath. So pause and breathe it all out.

3. Stuck—that feeling of not being able to move, of being rooted in somewhere you don't want to be, of wanting to move for-ward, perhaps "spinning your wheels" yet getting no traction. It may feel like a frustrated exhale, a huff of air that doesn't change anything. Exhale again.

Do any or all of these sound familiar? As I write them, they do for me. Strain, swirl, and stuck aren't states just experienced by us as indi-viduals. We also experience them in our relationships, in our teams, and in our organizations. They result in continued conflict, unproduc-tive meetings, failed strategic initiatives, and burnt out, disengaged, and overwhelmed contributors. These contributors have the potential to get great things done; they are just not in the states needed to make it happen.

When we find ourselves operating in the states of strain, swirl, or stuck, we do not have the influence or impact that we desire. We waste energy, getting caught up in the noise of busy work and busy lives, desiring to make a difference yet not doing so. Our experience is one of constantly running into roadblocks, obstacles, and conflicts—feeling like all our energy and effort is not getting us to where we want to go, the results we are after, the impact we desire, and the experience we want out of work and life.

Exhausted yet? This is the ultimate result when strain, swirl, or stuck continue unabated.

Despite this, there is something else also happening at the same time—a desire that keeps us moving forward through it all. And when we can connect to it is when transformation, influence, and impact happen. That something is potential.

THE POWER OF CONNECTING POTENTIAL

Potential is the possibility and capacity to develop or become—to make something happen. I have found, from working with and speaking to thousands of individuals, hundreds of teams, and dozens of organizations, a consistent theme. We have a deep need to bring it—potential—together and connect it. It is this force, this energy, *and* our desire and ability to connect it that is the catalyst and activator of personal and professional growth, deep learning, and transformed relationships, teams, families, and organizations.

The tile of this book is *Potential: How to Connect What's Already There for Exponential Impact* because its purpose is to guide you to connect yours. Throughout the book, I use the verbs *connect* and *connecting*, because if potential is the "thing," *connect* and *connecting* are the actions that make it real and tangible. While potential is often framed as something that we work toward over time with verbs like "realize," "reach," and "achieve," the biggest gift (and opportunity) of our potential comes from the fact that it is always there—ready to be connected in every moment. The present tense of *connect* tells us we can do it *right now.* And because we are never done developing or becoming, the "ing" of *connecting* speaks to it as a continuous opportunity and a powerful core practice that I will teach you in this book.

The problems of a VUCA world can cause our experience to be one of strain, swirl, or stuck—the Three *S*s. But when we *connect potential*, we experience the powerful impact of the "Three *E*s"—energy, ease, and effectiveness—regardless of the situation or circumstance we find ourselves in. As you read the short description of each of the *E*s, I again invite you to pause and experience each of them.

1. Energy—that feeling of vigor and vitality—a spark, force, or power that moves in and through us resulting in us having the dynamic experience of being animated and alive—moving us forward and inviting others to do the same.

2. Ease—that feeling of being unencumbered, moving with fluidity, flow, and freedom, where we experience progress without undue effort and things feel simple.

3. Effectiveness—that feeling of getting it done and done well, achieving success, intended results—being in a state to do great work and have positive impact.

Do any of these feel familiar? I hope and imagine that they do. I reconnected with the experience of each of these states as I put the words on the page, and it felt great. Together the states of energy, ease, and effectiveness are not only experienced by us in the moment, but they increase our influence and impact as well. Think about a time when you had energy and it flowed. When what you were doing was full of ease—easeful—and you were confident and effective. What was the influence and impact you had in the conversations you were part of? With your team members, your family, friends, and the task at hand? I imagine that it was both positive and productive. And that you not only had energy, ease, and effectiveness yourself but that it was contagious, resulting in the same experience for others around you. This book teaches you a simple yet powerful core practice to make connecting potential your way of being every day.

But that's not all. You will also learn how to leverage the exponential power of connecting potential because what I have also found through my years of living, working, and learning is that this thing called potential lives simultaneously in three dimensions—within us, between us, and around us:

> 1) *Within us* as individuals and the difference we desire to make in our worlds
>
> 2) *Between us* in our relationships and teams where the whole is greater than the sum of its parts
>
> 3) *Around us* in the organizational cultures and communities that we are constant contributors to and co-creators of whether we pay attention to them or not

And because each of these dimensions are connected to the others, when you influence and impact any one of them, you influence and impact every one of them. That is the exponential power of connecting potential!

WHY THIS BOOK IS DIFFERENT

There are lots of books written about the topics of individual potential, team performance, and organizational effectiveness—lots of really great books. I have read many of them and will share insights I have taken from them along with sources for further exploration. One of the challenges of reading a bunch of different books with a bunch of different frames of reference is that we are left to make connections between our insights to amplify their impact—connections that we don't always make.

Not with this book. Think of it as your one-stop read to empower you to connect potential in all three dimensions. More specifically you will:

✓ Optimize your Connect Potential Operating System. A small hint for now—no software or app download required!

✓ Hardwire a simple yet impactful three-part Connect Potential Core Practice.

✓ Activate the exponential influence and impact of the core practice in relationships, teams, and organizations.

✓ Apply your learning to both work and life because it's all connected, and as the mindfulness teacher Jon Kabat-Zinn says, "We are who we are wherever we go."

✓ Move forward with clarity and confidence on your connecting potential journey with additional support and guidance as a member of the Connecting Potential Community Hub where I share additional insights, inspirations, practices, tools, templates, and development programs with you. You can find a link to it at the end of the book.

Potential is more than an informative, interesting, and inspirational read. It is an invitation to interact and initiate action along the way. (I am also so excited that I managed to get an alliteration into the first chapter!) So the first invitation to interact is now:

Finish each of the following statements and answer the following questions either in your mind or out loud:

- "Location, location, ..."
- "Earth, wind, and ..."
- "lights, camera, ..."
- "Goldilocks and how many bears?
- How many little pigs?
- "I'll huff and I'll puff and I'll..."

What's the magic number? That's right—the magic number is three! Our brains like the number three because it is the smallest number of things that forms a pattern or a rhythm that can easily be hardwired. In the above example, two feels "incomplete" and the third word or statement completes it. Also, while the brain can remember seven things plus or minus two, it loves threes and likes fours (think phone numbers or credit card numbers).

In a world where there is way too much information coming at us to hold onto it all (much less do anything with it), this book uses the power of three to help you make it stick with the following core structure and elements:

One Mindset Shift (1)
One Operating System (2)
One Core Practice (3)
Three Dimensions for Exponential Impact!

You may have already felt the conversational tone of the book, and this tone is on purpose. Susan Scott, the author of *Fierce Conversations* and *Fierce Leadership*, says, "We are always involved in a conversation and sometimes it involves other people." I invite you to think of this book as a series of conversations that connect and build on each other.

Conversations that you will have with me as I share information, insights, inspirations, and stories. The words on the page will become a voice that interacts with you in conversation, guiding you on this journey of connecting potential.

Conversations that you will have with others as a result of what you read and learn. Throughout the book I provide prompts, powerful questions, practice activities, and conversation starters to help you apply, practice, and deepen your learning, developing connect potential muscles throughout your experience of the book.

And finally, the conversations that you will have with yourself along the way—perhaps the most important conversations of all. I will provide you with reflection prompts and simple activities to build self-conversation skills that connect potential in a variety of ways. I'll prompt you now and then to write something down or work something out in your journal. While it's up to you whether to do so, journaling is a useful tool for helping you connect your potential and track your journey through the book. Now is a great time to grab your favorite journal and reflect on the following *three* opening questions to help you focus your reading experience and plant the seeds for rich growth along the way. You can also order a downloadable companion journal with the activities and reflection prompts laid out for you at the Connecting Potential Community Hub.

www.connectingpotential.ca

1. What is one area in your work and life where your potential is there waiting to be connected (yet still isn't)?

2. What will be different when it is?

3. What is one small action you are committed to taking right now to make it happen? (Your answer might be, "Commit to the journey of this book.")

MEET YOUR CONVERSATION GUIDE

You are probably wondering, *Who is this person who will be having all these conversations with me and asking me all these questions?*

Let me formally introduce myself, your *Potential* author and conversation guide, Pam August. It is so wonderful to officially meet you!

Since that horrible "personality defect" conversation all those years ago, where I made the life-changing decision that led to a life of connecting potential and this conversation with you here right now, I have done a lot of learning along the way that I am so excited to share with you. This learning is built on a deep, formal foundation including an undergraduate degree in Adult Education, and a Masters of Arts in Leadership. As a lifelong learner, I have done a lot of learning in additional fields of expertise, including certifications in neuro-leadership coaching; organization and relationship systems coaching (ORSC, where I specialize in coaching teams); Brain Gym, the practice of educational kinesiology (simple movement to remove blocks and rewire our brains); and yoga teaching—a key personal practice to keep this energetic, sometimes-spiraling mind integrated, grounded, and connected.

My most significant learning has come through the experiences of my life and career which started as a fitness instructor and nutrition coach in the '80s, a college professor in the '90s and 2000s, and a developer of people potential at WestJet Airlines from 2004 to 2019, a global airline and one of Canada's most admired corporate cultures. There I held several roles including leadership development and coaching, team effectiveness coaching, and my final role as director of culture activation, where as a senior leader in the organization, my role was to keep my eyes, ears, and thumb on the pulse of this thing called "culture" across the whole organization and work with it to align it with WestJet's strategic direction. I left WestJet in January of 2019 and founded the powerful performance practice fittingly called Connecting Potential, where, as chief co-creator, I partner with vision-driven, purpose-led individuals, teams, and organizations who believe in the potential of people for real—meaning they are willing to do the real work every day to connect that potential for next-level, transformational results.

Now that some of the more "résumé" items are covered, let me share what I am about. In 2006, I was diagnosed with Crohn's disease, a serious illness that almost took my life—I lost forty pounds in forty days (forty pounds that I did not need to lose). I am happy to report that I live a very well-balanced life with this condition, as it created the potential for me to care for my health and well-being with commitment and consistency.

But during this initial flare that had me hospitalized for a week and off work for six months, I had a lot of time to reflect and re-reflect on what my purpose in work and life was. Part of this included reading the book *Let Your Life Speak* by Parker Palmer, an author, educator, and influential activist who focuses on issues in education, community, leadership, spirituality, and social change. Early in the book a simple and powerful notion of vocation and the importance of finding it jumped out at me that I paraphrase as "where our deep gladness meets the world's deep need."

It became clear to me that my deep gladness that met the world's deep need was to "create learning in relationship." It was what I did as a young child, as a twenty-three-year-old college student who had that epiphanic moment, and then as the learning professional, leader, wife, mom, and friend I am today. And this vocation, passion, at times obsession is now in service to the purpose of this book—to share with you what I have learned and continue to learn (because remember, we are never done or "there"). To share about the power of connecting potential to move through work and life with greater energy, ease, and effectiveness. This is what allows you to have the influence and impact you desire between yourself and others and around you in the organizations and communities that you are part of.

And here are some other things that "make me glad" so you get to know me a bit better and what you can expect in the flavor and experience of this book (chunked of course into three):

Crossing Edges

- **Really tricky problems**—the ones that "best practices" can't seem to solve because human systems are complex and unpredictable
- **Getting comfortable with being uncomfortable**—because that's where real learning happens
- **Getting s___ done**—a lot of meaningful stuff (what did you think the *s* was for?)

Creating Spaces

- **Listening deeply**—to what is being said and what wants to be heard so others feel safe to be real
- **Making meaning through challenge and chaos**—and moving forward together whether physically together or connected in other ways
- **Being a work in progress**—it really takes the pressure off

> *Leading with a Light Heart*
> - **Energy and dynamism**—physical, emotional, intellectual, spiritual—anything that moves me and moves others
> - **Learning always**—and in all ways
> - **Laughing**—a lot!

Finally, as I have already referenced, I have put my learning into action, connecting potential in a variety of contexts and challenges by working with and speaking to thousands of individuals, hundreds of teams, and dozens of organizations in Canada, the US, and across the globe with lasting learning and deep impact. Their stories bring the insights and practices I am going to share with you to life in real and relevant ways.

I love my work—I mean, really love it. I often say I am going to work until I am a hundred because I love what I do and spend too much money. In that order—or at least most of the time! This book is my opportunity to connect with many more amazing people including readers like you. Journeyers who want to bring together that thing inside, between, and around them—connecting potential! Now that you know what to expect in this journey and have met your guide, let's get started by getting into the right mindset to connect your potential.

POTENTIAL

ONE Mindset Shift

ONE Operating System

ONE Core Practice

THREE Dimensions of Exponential Impact

CHAPTER TWO

Grounding in the Right Mindset

Close your eyes for a moment. Okay, don't close them just yet—please read this short instruction first. As you have your eyes closed, think of these three things: an orange, a car, a beach. Now close your eyes and think of these three things. Once you've thought of each one, open our eyes.

Now ask yourself, *did I see the words orange, car, and beach?* The answer is most surely no. Instead, you saw an orange—was it peeled or unpeeled? If unpeeled, take a moment and peel the orange in your mind. Can you smell it now as well, even though there is not a peeled orange in front of you? Now think about the car again. What color is it? Red, silver, black? What type is it? Sports car, sport utility, 2001 Toyota Corolla? As it was probably not the 2001 Corolla, imagine it is a new purchase, and when you get into it, it has that "new car smell." And finally, the beach. Where is it? What is the texture of the sand? How warm is the sun? You might have noticed that your location feels a bit warmer, and you are craving a refreshing drink.

What this short experience just showed is this: the brain thinks in pictures and communicates in words a lot of the time. That is why you did not see the letters of the words, but rather you saw images of what the words represented. In fact, you likely saw more than the picture. You likely saw the object or put yourself in the experience of the thing and not only saw it, but experienced the sounds, smells, taste, and feel of it as well. This is the power of words. They create worlds in our minds, leading to one of my favorite sayings: *words create worlds* (Abraham Heschel). In the previous exercise, you weren't eat-ing an orange, driving a car, or sitting on a beach. You were still here in this book and yet had each of those three experiences. That is the power of words.

The words we use frame our mindset, and getting into a "potential" mindset is a foundational practice to connect it. The challenge is that we often spend too much time in a problem mindset. Let's experience the difference between the two, a problem mindset and a potential mindset, and how it shifts through the change of a word.

PROBLEM MINDSET VS. POTENTIAL MINDSET

Think about the word *problem* and notice what comes to mind. You might see a problem that you are currently experiencing—within yourself, with another person, or with a situation—a difficult colleague, a messy situation at work, an overfull inbox, or not enough hours in the day. See *problem* in your mind and notice the experience and emotions it conjures up. Name those emotions and notice the physical impact they have on you. Do you tense up? Does your breath speed up or do you momentarily hold your breath? Now exhale and shake it off—yes, physically shake it off. Did you know that humans are the only mammal that carries problems around them even when the problems aren't physically present? After a gazelle is chased by a predator and they outrun them, they stop, shake, and graze, letting the problem and accompanying stressful emotion go. So like Taylor Swift sings, "shake it off."

Now think about the word *potential* and notice what comes into your thinking. Again, you might see yourself, another person, or a situation—see a scene where potential is being connected: a goal has been achieved, a relationship has an important breakthrough, or a new learning insight has revealed itself to you. What is happening as you recall it and how does it feel? Name the emotions you are experiencing and the physical sensations that come with them. Do you feel more open? Is your breathing easier? Do you feel more energetic? Don't shake this off because the potential mindset and the states it evokes are ones that I want you to bring forward with your reading. This is what this book is all about—connecting potential. It starts with a mindset shift that is created by a world that is created by a word.

The above descriptions and distinctions are not to say that problems aren't real, don't exist, and don't need to be dealt with.

> It starts with a mindset shift that is created by a world that is created by a word.

One of the first questions I ask my clients is, "What is the problem that needs to be solved here?" The key is that when we are clear on what the problem is, not to stop there. The next step is to shift our mindset with our language by moving from *problem* to *potential.* For example, following up the *problem* question with ones something like this: "What do I want to happen here?" "What is the potential here?" "What is possible from here?" "What does success (potential) look like?" If you already do this—yay! Now you know why this is a powerful practice, and it is one of many that you will deepen through this book. If not, you now have your first action to connect potential—shift your mindset by shifting your language—in this case from *problem* to *potential* because it is a critical first step.

As an example, as I originally wrote these words, I was living the impact of a problem mindset and the reality of how the words I was saying to myself were creating it. My husband and I are fortunate to have a seasonal home in Prince Edward Island (PEI) on the East Coast of Canada—our happy place since 2008. Living on the shore comes with risk in addition to rewards, and this risk became a reality as Hurricane Fiona hit PEI with a swift and devastating impact while I was on the other side of the country working with clients.

However, this story is less about the impact of the hurricane, and more about the problem mindset the words I told myself created and kept me in long after the storm passed. *"All our hard work and sweat and tears into our happy place has been wiped away." "It will never be the same again." "Maybe it is not worth it." "We should have known better than to have a home so close to the shore." "It will just happen again." "Why are you so upset by this when others clearly have much more difficult and traumatic challenges to deal with every day?"* These are just some examples of the words I was telling myself to create the problem mindset I experienced from over 4500 km away. I felt anxious, defeated, guilty, and distracted by focusing on things that I *couldn't* control, instead of something that I *could* control and create—sharing my learning with you in this story. The good news is that you reading this story now is evidence that I worked through my problem mindset, made a shift, and connected the potential in the situation.

> I felt anxious, defeated, guilty, and distracted by focusing on things that I *couldn't* control, instead of something that I *could* control and create—sharing my learning with you in this story.

Here is what I did: I noticed that I was in a problem mindset of my own making and that my words were keeping me in the states of strain, stuck, and swirl all at the same—a hurricane of my own creation! I then remembered that the point I wanted to make in this part of the book is that we have the power to shift our mindsets by shifting our words, so I did just that by asking myself the question, "What is the potential that my problem mindset is creating, and what is possible from here?" The first thought that came to me was that it is okay to not be okay when tough things happen.

When we notice what we are saying to ourselves and the mindset and states that our words are creating, it allows us to consciously shift them by choosing different words that create different worlds, creating the mindset conditions for potential to be connected. By asking what was possible, I no longer lamented what was lost, instead focusing on what mattered most and what could now be (potential). The magic of PEI extends far beyond beautiful shorelines and pretty gardens—at its core it is about the amazing people and communities that make up the island and the possibility for us to rebuild together (which is what we did). The hurricane still happened, our property was still destroyed—what was different was my experience of the situation by shifting my mindset from problem to potential.

I realize at this point in the book that there are two things that I may need to clarify and build out further—my perspectives on the words *potential* and *problem*. When I use the word *potential* in this book, I use it in the context of what we want, what we want to move toward, or what wants to happen in a positive way. I also want to stress here that problems in and of themselves are not negative. In fact, if you are like me, tackling a juicy, messy problem may be just what you want to take on to connect your potential—a.k.a. "I love a good challenge"—and activate your best thinking, feeling, and action. When I refer to a problem or potential mindset, I am referring to the dynamic and repeating cycle that we create for ourselves and others resulting in either the experience of strain, swirl, and stuck, or energy, ease, and effectiveness.

Think about where you might be caught in a problem mindset right now—stuck, strained, or swirling—and ask yourself, "What are the words that I am saying to myself that are creating the problem world I find myself in?" Then ask yourself, "What words can I say to myself to create a world or mindset of potential?" Take a moment and make the shift right now as you read these words. What is the potential for you in the problem mindset you find yourself in? What is possible from here? Notice any shift in mindset, make a journal entry, and then breathe in and breathe out before we do one more thing to ground ourselves for the connecting potential exploration ahead—connect or reconnect with what matters most to you.

GROUNDING OUR MINDSET WITH WHAT MATTERS MOST

Through the disruption and difficulty of the pandemic (remember March 2020, then shake it off), I noticed I was hearing the word *matter* being used a lot and became curious about what it meant. Through my research—in this case, going to "the Google"—I found several definitions and descriptions of this thing called matter, that I synthesized into the following one:

> **Matter** *n.*
>
> Some "**thing**" of **substance** and/or **significance**.

The three bolded words, *thing, substance,* and *significance,* stood out to me because together they capture why "mattering matters." First off, matter is a thing, a substance that makes something tangible. We can see it, feel it, and experience it in a real way. Imagine right now that you are holding matter in your hand. For some reason the matter I imagine in my hand is Silly Putty (perhaps because I loved its unique smell as a child). Reflect for a moment on the matter, the thing in your hand, and experience how matter is a real thing. Now I would like you to think of something that is significant to you. This "thing," while more abstract (for example, you may have thought of family, learning, or adventure), is something that matters to you.

Next, I invite you to look around the space that you are in and let your eyes land on an object with substance, some "thing," some matter. If possible, you may also want to place it in your hand. The thing that my eyes landed on is a set of three metal starbursts on my coffee table. Now that your eyes have landed on this matter, reflect on your answer to this question: "How does this object (substance) represent something in my life that matters (is of significance)?" For me, this trio of starburst sculptures represents family because they were one of the last gifts that I gave my mom before she passed away in 2016. We both always loved surrounding ourselves with beautiful things, and this trio reminds me of her and our shared passions. And it makes me smile every time I look at it.

Your turn now. Go back to the object and ask yourself, "How does this object represent something in my life that is of significance?" The connection that you make may be more literal, for example you be looking at a picture of family (human or furry), or more metaphoric like with my starburst example. Notice next your experience of connecting with something that matters to you and reflect on how it both grounds you and your mindset in the moment. That is the power of what matters and why I have invited you into this experience at the beginning of our journey together. I encourage you to make note of it in your journal and each day take a moment to connect with *matter* that reminds you what *matters*, particularly when things get challenging and problematic.

What we just did together is also my favorite ice-breaker conversation for groups I work with. I call it "Objects of Mattering." There is something powerful that happens when we make a connection between physical *matter* and mental and emotional *mattering* that quickly connects people in a richer, more meaningful conversation than if I had just said, "Tell the group about something that matters to you."

You can find instructions to share it with others on the Community Hub as a member of this powerful community and movement. As I previously shared, you can find insights, inspirations, resources, and tools to both broaden and deepen your capacity to connect your potential and help others do the same!

Now that we have our mindsets where they need to be to connect potential, let's dive into the dimensions where potential lives—within us as individuals, between us in our relationships and teams, and around us in cultures.

POTENTIAL

ONE Mindset Shift

From *Problem* to *Potential*,
grounding in what matters

ONE Operating System

ONE Core Practice

THREE Dimensions of Exponential Impact

CHAPTER THREE

Potential in 3-D

THE THREE DIMENSIONS OF POTENTIAL

In 2014, I attended a theatre production in Charlottetown, PEI, titled *Story.* This play was a celebration of the rich storytelling traditions of the island and how they continue to shape its warm and connected culture. The narrator of the play was appropriately named "Story," and as he welcomed us into the experience, he said something that I have never forgotten: **"Story costumes fact, bringing it to greater awareness."**

This statement captures the power of story, making facts more visible and visceral, more present and palpable. I started this book with my story to make this thing called connecting potential more than an interesting concept and to make it real. As we explore the three dimensions of potential—within us, between us, and around us—I will continue sharing my story along with those of other potential connectors I have worked with along the way.

WITHIN US

Not only did that horrific "you have a personality defect" conversation result in a path that led me to my husband and the family we co-created, it also led me back to a pivotal career opportunity to connect the potential within myself three years later when I was hired to teach in the program that I graduated from. In an interesting twist to the story, a position opened up because the instructor who devastated me left the program. This program focused on nutrition and food service management, and my claim to fame when teaching in it was that I never got to teach a course that any students wanted to take. I taught human relations to allied health professionals who were more focused on learning procedures than patient interaction, and I taught nutrition and food safety to hospitality professionals and chefs who wanted the four food groups to be salt, sugar, grease, and alcohol (spoiler alert—they aren't, although coffee should make the cut!). This meant that I needed to get creative in how to make the learning compelling and something that students could see potential in for themselves. While my energy and enthusiasm for the subject areas I taught often engaged my students in the moment, the problem with my approach became apparent early on.

I was teaching nutrition and food safety to my first cohort of hotel management students in my first semester of teaching. They were an energetic, raucous group as we would expect hospitality professionals to be with their energy matching mine, making for great classroom sessions. I was teaching, and they were learning—or so I thought until the results of the mid-term exam came back where more than half the class failed it! I was devastated and immediately started blaming myself for this failure and lack of learning. My thoughts were swirling, building up the problem I was creating in my mind with each rotation. Not only was this a failure, my problem mindset quickly turned me into *the* failure.

Thankfully, my observant teaching partner saw my distress and gave me a simple and sage piece of advice: "Before you give the exams back, ask the class how they prepared for it." I went into class Monday morning after a weekend of ruminating with my firmly entrenched problem mindset, took a deep breath, and asked that important question about how my students prepared themselves for the exam. The class's immediate response was to burst out laughing—that's right, they laughed. This was followed up by statements like, "I was at bar. I didn't even look at my notes. I was still drunk when I took the test." I realized that the class had mistaken my light-hearted, energetic approach for low standards. My standards are anything but low—a fact that my husband and sons can fully attest to! The insight that appeared in that moment was that I needed to bring both challenge and support to my teaching, and what I had been doing was too heavily weighted on the support side. The potential connected in that moment was the beginning of me becoming a powerful facilitator of learning (more on this later).

We often hear the language of potential being used in the context of individuals. Phrases like, "living up to their potential," "not achieving their potential," and "reaching potential" are ways to describe the actions of potential within

> The potential connected in that moment was the beginning of me becoming a powerful facilitator of learning

us as individuals. While the word *potential* in each of these statements is abstract and intangible, when it is connected, the outcome and impact is tangible: the achievement of an athletic milestone, completion of a program, pushing through a challenge, developing new and/or deeper learning. In my case, the potential connected within me was becoming an instructor that intentionally brought both challenge and support to my teaching, resulting in real and deep learning. *And* sharing this learning now with all of you. Take a moment to reflect and journal on this question: where in your work and life could you more intentionally balance challenge and support for greater potential connection?

In all cases, the potential within us is this "thing" that is intangible yet present and that connects to result in something tangible with positive result and impact. And this something—our potential—and the desire to connect is what keeps us striving to learn, grow, and develop, even when it is tough. And as a reminder, we are never done growing, learning, developing. That's why this action of connecting potential is a powerful lifelong catalyst when we hardwire it through practice as a way of being and doing.

This was the story for our oldest son, Cayden, who fell in love with hockey during his first-ever minor hockey tryout. When I say fell in love, I mean literally fell, as this was also the first time our nine-year-old "hockey player" ever had on equipment and skates, barely standing up on the ice, much less playing the game of hockey. I will never forget the side-eye glare my mom gave me as we watched him stumble around the ice with the occasional crash into the boards to stop himself amongst other skilled players whose parents hadn't committed the Canadian sin of not getting their children on skates as soon as they were out of diapers. At the end of the tryout, as he was coming off the ice, I put on my best encouraging-yet-tentative mom smile and asked, "Well, honey, how was it—did you have fun?" He looked up at me, grinned, and said, "I suck, but I love it and I'll get better!" He did, he did, and he did.

Hockey turned out to be one of his biggest loves and his biggest challenges. As his skill increased, the play became more serious, and the reality that all is not fair in the politics of team sport became far too real. While over the years he experienced strain, swirl, and stuck, for him, what was in the way became the way (remember Lao Tzu), and he stayed committed to connecting his potential through it all, becoming the best player that he could be and now using his learning and passion for the sport to coach players to connect their potential along with getting out on the outdoor rink as soon as the water freezes. The determination and resilience that he built through the sport also served to connect his potential in many other ways. He is now a PhD student whose research focuses on the intersection of applied mathematics and computer and neuroscience and a teaching assistant who is known for his commitment to modeling learning excellence. Proud mom over here!

While the circumstances of these two stories are different, they both illustrate that this thing called connecting potential within us is not something that happens to us—it is something that we do with what happens. And it is not a one and done, a place that we reach and stay—it is a continuous action, a practice of connecting again and again.

I invite you now to take a moment and think of one of your stories about connecting potential within you. Jot down your answers to these questions in your journal.

> Connecting potential within us is not something that happens to us—it is something that we do with what happens.

- When was a time that you connected potential within you?

- What were the circumstances, and what was your experience of them?

- What did you do, and what was the impact?

I also invite you to notice your experience as you recall it now—what are you thinking, feeling, and doing as a result? I hope that you notice you already know how to do the thing that this book is teaching you to do. The teachings, stories, and experiences that I am sharing with you serve to build on the connect potential "muscle memory" you already have, making these muscles even stronger for greater energy, ease, and effectiveness in accessing them moving forward.

BETWEEN US

The second dimension of potential is between us—in our relationships and teams. Let's go back to the story of my students' mid-term exam results, where I knew I needed to connect the potential of "challenge and support" as their instructor. Immediately after I had this insight, I shared it with my hospitality management students. Their uncomfortable nodding and breaking of eye contact told me that I was right about not providing enough challenge and that they knew the balance between challenge and support was about to change. The very next day I started the practice of beginning each class with a five-question quiz that became a small part of their mark and a big part of a shift in the potential between us as instructor and learning community—and yes, within them as individuals as they also showed up differently after the shift within me. I called the quiz "In It to Win It" because basically all students had to do to be successful was show up to class (be in it) and pay attention to key learning (win it).

While I knew that this quiz would result in more students showing up on time to class and engaging more actively in their learning, what I didn't anticipate was how much it would change the potential of the relationship between us to become deeper and more dynamic. You see, my students wanted to be challenged, unconsciously at first and then consciously after my shift. And when I didn't challenge them, they not only didn't perform, they felt let down. Not only did they get "in it to win it," we became co-creators in the experience. We all provided challenge and support to each other, making them stronger learners and me a more effective instructor. Students started providing me with more feedback on what was working and what wasn't, with constructive suggestions on how to make the learning more real and relevant for them, and I responded. This resulted in the group's capstone experience where small learning groups chose a restaurant menu to analyze the nutritional value of the menu and made recommendations to increase it, still making it something that guests would want to purchase. Not only did they choose a menu to focus on, on their initiative, they decided as learning groups to go dine at the restaurant together to have the full experience. It became a project that future cohorts heard stories about and looked forward to learning from—"we actually get to go out for dinner in our nutrition class!"

As I reflect on this story, I'm reminded of the quote from Aristotle: "The whole is greater than the sum of its parts." This is a great description of the "between us" dimension of potential. It reminds us that something exists between us that is more than each of us as individuals. Again, this something is potential, and when we connect it we tap into the energy and intelligence that lives between us, which includes the energy and intelligence that is each of us and becomes something more. Now it's your turn. Grab your journal and think about a time when you worked with another person or in a team that helped you accomplish something that you couldn't on your own.

- What did it feel like? Was the experience energetic and easeful?

- How did it feel to accomplish something as a team rather than an individual?

- How was the whole more than the sum of its parts?

That feeling of "I couldn't have done it without you!" is what happens when we connect potential between us. This can be between a leader and team member as they break through a lingering challenge or problem together, or a team that completes a big project together, or an instructor and her learners who become partners and co-creators of the learning process. Perhaps the best example of connecting potential between us is in the world of sport, where the team of "no superstars" beats the team that has technically more skilled players because of the chemistry (the potential) that they create between them.

Not only is the tangible result something that could not have been achieved by each person on their own, but the experience of doing it together is one where the energy and ease of the "between us" dynamic builds on itself. This was what happened in that nutrition class all those years ago and in the next story.

Connecting the potential between us often results because of difficulty rather than despite it, as was the case between a former leader and myself through a really difficult situation and conversation. I was working as an individual contributor developing and coaching leaders. A sudden change in the team prompted my leader to ask me if I would step in and support by managing the leadership development team in addition to the work I was doing. Even though I had avoided formal management roles most of my career because I identified more strongly with the practice of the work (that is, learning and development), I respected my leader and wanted to help however I could. So I said yes to the request.

While I was effective in some aspects of managing the team, it was clear that this was not the right role for me, at least not at that time. My leader and I sat down to have "the conversation" about it. While difficult to have, it was a very different conversation than the one I first shared in this book—the "personality defect" one—because of what already lived between us in our relationship. My leader and I shared respect and appreciation—and the potential that we discovered between us was that we could co-create more effectively with me in a different role. My leader was clear and genuine in expressing what I brought to the team—and what was missing. In that moment because she was balancing both challenge and support, I responded by saying that I didn't care what role I was in and only wanted to be of greatest service to the team and the organization. We then aligned on how we would position me for the greatest positive impact, in a senior individual contributor role, and how we would continue partnering and co-creating, each bringing our individual strengths. Her noticing and appreciation of what I brought (support) and honesty in what I didn't (challenge) and my open response to what she shared also created the conditions for me to powerfully connect my potential. It helped me contribute at a higher, more impactful and influential level and created a dynamic between us where we achieved things together that neither of us could have done on our own. It required both of us to connect potential between us.

She continues to be an influential leader as a people and culture executive for a global organization and is one of my clients. Together we challenge and support each other as female leaders and connectors of potential between us in significant and impactful ways. Yes, when the potential between us is connected, the whole is greater than the sum of its parts.

AROUND US

To understand the third dimension of potential, let's return one more time to my story about the hospitality management program. So far, I have shared how the potential *within* me connected to become an instructor who dynamically balanced challenge and support, and how my learners and I connected the potential *between* us to co-create impactful learning experiences neither of us could have done on our own. Over several years of repeating this pattern of challenge, support, and co-creation again and again, the course gained a reputation of being an impactful learning lab. I started hearing more and more from students coming in that they knew that the way learning happened in this class was unique, with words like "collaborative," "energizing," and "deep." I didn't consciously know it at the time, but what they were experiencing, contributing to, and talking about was the learning culture that was constantly being co-created by connecting the potential around us. One of my proudest moments as a college instructor at SAIT was when I was awarded a provincial teaching award for "excellence in promoting student learning" through this course. The most gratifying part of the award is that it was student-initiated and my nominators were a mixed group of learners from different years and different cohorts. While I was the one who received the award, I was very aware that there was a dynamic that had been created in the course that was beyond myself and these specific learners. It was the culture of the program and the potential that was constantly connected around those of us who were in it. At a recent keynote, I reconnected with one of the students from that program. They shared with me that this powerful learning culture shaped their co-creation approach to leadership as an executive in the hospitality industry.

Peter Drucker, author and influential thinker on management, is famously quoted as saying, "Culture eats strategy for breakfast." This statement speaks to the power of the potential that lives around us in organizational cultures—or more specifically when it's not connected and becomes an obstacle to strategy execution. It is the real, yet often hard to get a handle on, third dimension of potential and the topic of much organizational assessment, research, and writing in business. When I work with organizations in the culture space, I often use the metaphor of water, culture being the water that we find ourselves in. And much like fish in water, we don't even know that we are in it. We can feel it the moment we walk into a space or read about an organization and want to be part of that "thing," but we can't put our finger on what we are experiencing or why it makes us feel the way it does. Later in the book I will demystify this experience by making clear what culture is, what it isn't, and how to connect the potential around you for greater effectiveness and a better experience at work. For now, a story about WestJet and Simon Sinek that speaks to the power of the potential around us.

When I worked at WestJet, one of my yearly initiatives was to be the lead designer and facilitator of our annual leadership summits. When I took over this portfolio of work, the events had great content but weren't always connected to developing the culture needed to execute on WestJet's strategy priorities. I saw what was missing and shifted the summits from disconnected conference events to sessions that built on the organization's previous year's learning and were a catalyst for the next year of work ahead, focusing on the critical connection between strategy and culture.

It was 2011, and I like millions of people was discovering the powerful messages and impact of Simon Sinek on YouTube with his Ted Talk, "How Great Leaders Inspire Action" and from his book *Start with Why*. I reached out to Speaker's Spotlight, a speaking bureau who represents Simon (and now represents me) to book a call with him about our upcoming summit. I did not want to have him come and speak to our six hundred leaders, but rather to meet at a studio so I could interview him on video and share it with all nine thousand of our WestJetters. We got Simon on the conference call, and when I shared my request, his immediate response was, "You could just watch my Ted Talk for free." I clarified that we wanted him to speak specifically to WestJetters because we were an organization that believed in our *why* of enriching the lives of everyone in WestJet's world and, at this critical juncture in our airline's history, really needed to lean into it with targeted teachings.

We went around on this for a bit, until Simon made me a counteroffer, which was this: if I would bring three or four WestJetters who emulated our *why* from across the business for him to interview after I interviewed him, he would do it. It was a quick "yes," and our conference theme became "Start with Why." In October of 2011, we met with him and a film crew in a Brooklyn loft for the conversations to happen. It still stands as one of my peak experiences from my time at WestJet because as I watched Simon interview our WestJetters—our president, an aircraft maintenance engineer, a customer service agent, and a project manager from IT—the potential was so clear. It was around us in our culture, not only because of what these amazing WestJetters and thousands of others were doing as individuals and in their teams, but because it was there "in the water." It created the conditions and catalyst for our purpose and potential of enriching lives to connect again and again. At the end of the interviews, Simon observed the following: "To be a WestJetter it is about what can we do together. We, not I—*I, me, my* should be banned from this organization—we, together, us are essential components to its culture." He then finished with *the* statement that captured the essence of WestJet's culture and the potential connecting around us by saying, "WestJet starts with *We.* I am sure that you noticed this, right? The most important word in WestJet is *We.* It's literally the first two letters of your name. It's not that the airline comes first; people come first."

The funny thing is that at the time, none of us noticed it because it was the water that *we* all swam in together. When you joined WestJet, you didn't just get a job there, you became a *WestJetter,* a member of this special swim team. "WestJet Starts with We" became the theme for the leadership summit the following year.

Take a moment now to think about a place that you have worked at or experienced as a customer where you admired and appreciated their culture. Now dive into the water that this organization swims in, and ask yourself, what three words best describe the culture of the organization? While I have no idea what your words are, I imagine that you were able to come up with them quite quickly, in doing so naming the potential that is being connected and co-created around everyone who is part of it. Now ask yourself and write in your journal, what three words do I want to describe the culture around me now?

INDICATORS OF CONNECTING POTENTIAL IN EACH DIMENSION

So that's the introduction to the three dimensions of potential, where I hope that the stories I shared effectively costumed the facts about them, bringing them to greater awareness for you. We will come back to the dimensions later in the book. I want to end this chapter by giving you some helpful indicators for when potential is being connected in each of the three dimensions and when it isn't. As you read it, ask yourself to what extent you experience any of these indicators. What has been and is the impact? Feel free to grab your journal and jot down anything that comes to mind.

WITHIN US	
Connected Potential Indicators	Disconnected Potential (Problem Indicators)
▪ You have a sense of accomplishment. ▪ You achieve things that you didn't know or think were possible a short time ago. ▪ You know that you are achieving something different than before. ▪ Although you have worked hard, you have energy or the experience of what I call "good tired." ▪ You look back on the experience and smile. ▪ You look forward to the next challenge. ▪ You have energy, ease, and effectiveness (three Es) and influence and impact.	▪ You find yourself pointing fingers at others rather than looking in the mirror. ▪ You use words like "I can't," "I failed," "I shouldn't." ▪ You think, "Why bother? It didn't work last time." ▪ Your excuses not to take action are more appealing than your reasons to take it. ▪ You look outside of yourself rather inside yourself for solutions. ▪ You are hard on yourself. ▪ You regret past actions or worry about future ones. ▪ Your experience is strain, stuck, swirl (three Ss).

BETWEEN US	
Connected Potential Indicators	*Disconnected Potential (Problem Indicators)*
<ul><li>We acknowledge and appreciate that we couldn't have done it on our own.</li><li>We use "we" and "us."</li><li>We high-five physically or metaphorically.</li><li>We surpass what we thought was possible on our own.</li><li>We celebrate rather than criticize each other.</li><li>We lean into conflict because we know it will make us better.</li><li>Our experience is energy, ease, and effectiveness (the three Es) and influence and impact.</li></ul>	<ul><li>Team/relationship members blame others for shortcomings.</li><li>We use "they" and "them"</li><li>We say things like, "It's not my responsibility."</li><li>We would rather do it ourselves because we can do it better and then get mad because others aren't pulling their own weight.</li><li>We avoid conflict because it will lead nowhere good.</li><li>Our experience is strain, stuck, swirl (the three Ss).</li></ul>

AROUND US	
Connected Potential Indicators	*Disconnected Potential (Problem Indicators)*
<ul><li>We run to work rather than away from it (at least most of the time!).</li><li>We look forward to the start of the work week.</li><li>We think about our organization with appreciation and pride.</li><li>While we put in a lot, we feel that we get it back and more.</li></ul>	<ul><li>Members "quit" even though they stay (disengaged).</li><li>The culture feels "toxic."</li><li>Members believe that culture is something that someone else needs to create.</li><li>There is no appreciation for or pride in the organization.</li><li>Leaving work on a Friday is the best moment of a bad week.</li></ul>

• We have breakthroughs and set new standards in the industry we are in. • We see ourselves as important contributors and co-creators in the culture we are part of. • Our organization has energy, ease, and effectiveness (three Es) and influence and impact.	• Members feel the organization is working against them. • Going to work feels like an energy-sucking vortex. • We see ourselves as separate from the experience we are having in the culture we are part of, and rather than contribute, we consume. • The organizational experience is strain, stuck, swirl (three Ss).

As you reviewed these three tables, you were likely able to think of examples and relate to indicators from both columns. I know that as I wrote them, I certainly did because I have lived each of them. And in more cases than I would like to admit I was slow to practice what I will teach in this book, staying stuck in a problem mindset and "three S" states far too often. Each time I shifted my mindset and my action, what was in the way did become the way. My goal for you, my reader, is to learn from my learning and speed up the process of connecting potential in all three dimensions.

POTENTIAL IN 3D FOR EXPONENTIAL IMPACT

I hope that by now are you are seeing that when you connect potential, you have greater impact and influence in work and in life, while experiencing greater energy, ease, and effectiveness.

To quickly recap what's been shared so far about the three dimensions: when we connect potential within ourselves, we achieve things that we didn't know were possible for us. When we connect it between us, we have stronger, more productive, high-performing, and fulfilling relationships one-on-one and in the teams that we are part of. And finally, when we connect it around us in organizations that we are members of, we are key co-creators of cultures that we are proud of and that others want to be a part of and contribute to.

And if that all sounds great, there is one more piece of good news! When we influence any one dimension, we influence all dimensions because they are all connected, and we are all connected. That is the exponential, or what I sometimes call (x)potential, impact of connecting potential. In the stories that I shared in this chapter, when potential was connected in any one of the dimensions it resulted in potential connecting in the other two just because of their connection.

This is the exponential power we unlock when we connect potential because it doesn't matter what dimension it happens in, it just matters that it happens. Let's continue learning and experiencing why this bold statement is true, but first dive into the operating system that makes it all possible. The great news is that you don't need to download an app or software, because this operating system is *you*!

POTENTIAL

ONE Mindset Shift

**From *Problem* to *Potential*,
grounding in what matters**

ONE Operating System

ONE Core Practice

THREE Dimensions of Exponential Impact

Within us as individuals
Between us in our relationships and teams
Around us in the cultures we co-create and contribute to

CHAPTER FOUR

Your Connect Potential Operating System

I hope you are glad that this next chapter requires no technology or fancy tools because I sure am! While I use the language of operating system because it is one that we all can relate to, our operating system—our nervous system with the brain as the central piece—is more complex and magical than the most "whiz-bang" software or technology could ever be. As well, in our high-tech yet low-touch, hyper-connected yet disconnected, information-full yet insight-poor world, I want you to be reassured right from the start that you have everything that you need to operate from a place of potential, making powerful connections along the way without any added tech. Let's dive in and discover how together.

As I think about this next concept, the image of a television program that I watched as a kid comes to mind, *ABC Afterschool Special*. My favorite episodes were ones where we dove into the body, taking a journey through the science in a real and visceral way, exploring the parts with a sense of curiosity and adventure. That is the type of journey that I am taking you on now as we dive into the three-part Connect Potential Operating System, so I invite you to bring along your curiosity as well. The lens through which our exploration will happen is one of learning, behavior, and performance rather than in-depth neuroscience. I will layer in relevant insights from the field of neuroscience as they are useful to understanding how your operating system works to help or hinder your ability to connect potential through your action, feeling, and thinking.

IT'S ABOUT THE BRAIN-BODY CONNECTION

The exploration of our Connect Potential Operating System starts by looking at the brain, an organ seated within our skull, the size of a large grapefruit and about three pounds. Our operating system, however, is much more than our "above the ears" brain. Neuroscience clearly shows that the human brain is part of a dynamic interconnected system in the whole body via the nervous system. Neurons, the cells that make up the nervous system, are found throughout the body. So when you hear sayings like "trust your heart" or "go with your gut," there is a scientific basis for them. Dr. Andrew Huberman, tenured professor at Stanford School of Medicine and founder of the Huberman Labs podcasts, further explains that the language of the nervous system is electricity. The electrical activity between our neurons dictates our lives. That is a powerful statement (pun intended). And when we consider that our brains map to all parts of our body, the resources we have available to connect potential expand even more via the brain-body connection.

I first became fascinated with the brain-body connection when I was acutely aware that mine was disconnected in my early twenties. It was then that I became clear that I lived with significant depression and anxiety. You see, at the time that I was told I had a "personality defect" that would prevent me from being successful in life, I already believed it to be true, because I was deep into a cycle of clinical depression. While on the outside, I appeared to be fine—more than fine, actually, because I was trying to compensate for my distress—on the inside I was more than strained, swirling, and stuck. I was completely disconnected, fragmented, anxious, and deeply, profoundly sad. I compensated for my distress and disconnection by pleasing, performing, and perfecting even more. This led many wonderful health providers—doctors, social workers, psychiatrists, and psychologists—to believe that I was fine, when I was not. They thought I was getting through it, when really I was sinking deeper. Everyone else saw me moving forward, while I could barely hold myself and my breath together standing where I was.

While I was dealing with the attacks from my instructor, which were nothing compared to how I beat myself up inside, I connected with a psychologist who visited our nutrition program to talk about learning styles. She not only became my healer—I believe my work with her over the years saved my life—she guided me through a deep learning journey that included powerful talk therapy and went much deeper into the wisdom of my body. That journey introduced me to life-changing brain-body tools that then became part of my professional learning as a licensed Brain Gym instructor. (More on this powerful method later.)

I share my personal struggles with you as a reminder again that our deepest difficulties are also the opportunities for the deepest connections of potential. That is, when we do the work of connecting it. It's also to show you that the Connect Potential Operating System is more than interesting theory. It comes from the synthesis of knowledge in several fields and is grounded in real lived experience. So let's dive in!

THE "HAND MODEL" OF YOUR BRAIN

It's no secret that the working of the whole human brain—including those billions of neurons throughout your body—is complex beyond the complete comprehension of even the most brilliant neuroscientist. The good news? Understanding the core functions that it performs as an *operating system* can be made quite simple.

> Our operating system is designed for us to do three things: to act, to feel, and to think.

Our operating system is designed for us to do three things: **to act, to feel, and to think**. Let's explore how this happens using Dr. Dan Siegel's hand model of the brain. I have found his model to be the most accessible and understandable one because it uses something we have with us every day, our hands. Plus, it maps nicely to the Connect

Potential Operating System. And it makes for a great party trick at your next social gathering! Quick note: this is not intended to be an in-depth brain study so I have provided a reference list for further exploration of this topic in the bibliography and on the Community Hub.

I had the opportunity to learn in person with Dr. Siegel at the Mindful Society Summit in 2018 and have since read many of his books and adopted several of his mindfulness practices. Dr. Siegel is an MD, psychiatrist, scientist, therapist, and a leading mind in the field of mindfulness. He created the hand model of the brain to make its working clear and easy to understand. The good news is you don't have to be a neuroscientist to understand these concepts. The key to unlocking them is in the palm of your hand. What follows is my summary and paraphrase of his practical model. For the more visually minded, you can search "Dr. Siegel's hand model of the brain" for the images of what I describe.

PART 1: BRAIN STEM = ACTION

Hold this book in one of your hands. Then hold out your other hand in front of you with your palm open toward you. The hand in front of you represents your brain. As you look back and forth between your outstretched hand and this page, I want you to notice that your hand is connected to your body just like your brain is. This connection in your hand-model brain is just below the wrist. Think of your arm bones like your spinal column, the primary connection point between your above-your-ears brain and your body.

Now look at your wrist and the base of your palm. This represents the *brain stem*, which is responsible for the automatic functions essential for survival, like maintaining your core body temperature, your heartbeat, breathing, and other involuntary functions and movement. The brain stem is also the above-your-ears brain's first line of communication with the body so sensory and motor information can travel between them.

These functions are necessary for us to survive and to take action. Remember the statement, "The body always wins," because it holds particular importance when it comes to connecting potential, as I will explain throughout the book.

PART 2: LIMBIC BRAIN = FEELING

Now hold your hand brain with your palm open and facing you, folding your thumb into the middle of your palm. Your thumb and where it now sits represents the second part of Dr. Siegel's hand model of the brain, the *limbic system*. I also refer to this part as the "heart of the brain" because it is both in the middle and also the part most closely associated with emotion, the feeling part of your operating system.

Notice that the limbic brain is connected to the brain stem, and they work together to influence aspects of behavior, emotions, and physiological responses. The limbic brain works in part to motivate and drive action in the brain stem through the processing and regulating of emotions physically—like breathing, heart rate, and alertness.

Now look at the knuckle where your thumb attaches to your hand. While not an anatomically correct representation, this knuckle represents an important part of the brain's limbic system—the amygdala. The amygdala is sometimes referred to as the emotional "hot button" in the brain because its job is to look for threats and trigger a reaction in the brain stem if one is detected. Think of this like your "fight or flight" response and reflexive action—action that sometimes in retrospect was not such a great idea. For example, some might also say that this hot button is hardwired to a specific hand gesture when we are cut off in traffic—not that I have personal experience with that one. Although the amygdala evolved at a time in human history where threats were generally physical, often life-or-death ones, today it does not differentiate between threats that are physical or psychological, real or imagined. Perhaps the best example of this for many of us is when someone asks us the often-dreaded question, "Can I give you some feedback?"

Why the dread? According to Dr. David Rock, creator of the neuro-leadership model, the brain-based one-on-one coaching methodology I am certified in, the triggered "amygdala hijack" that results from that question creates the same emotional and physiological reaction as when you suddenly hear footsteps behind you in a dark alley at night. I will let that one sink in. Hearing we are about to receive some feedback feels the same as a threat in a dark alley at night. Real, imagined, physical, psychological, it doesn't matter to the amygdala—a threat is a threat, and its job is to let the brain stem know it's time to act.

The limbic system is not just about threat and reaction. This is the part of the brain as well where we feel and form emotional connection or bonding. Take a moment and think about someone who matters to you. Not only do you see them, it is likely that you feel something, and you may be smiling. Finally, the limbic system is also integral in the creation of learning and memory because the limbic system ascribes meaning and attaches a feeling to our experiences as they go into long-term storage to be retrieved consciously or unconsciously later. Let's quickly experience this by recalling a situation with the worst leader you ever worked with—then quickly shake it off! Next recall the best leader you have ever worked with and notice the shift in emotion. Hold onto those feelings as we look at the third part of the hand model of the brain—the *cortex*.

PART 3: CORTEX = THINKING

If you are playing along physically, pick your hand up again, because I know you put it down (I know that because I did too). Place your thumb back into the middle of your palm with your palm facing you. Now curl your fingers over the thumb to form a loose fist. What you have just created is the third part of Dr. Siegel's hand model of the brain, the cortex where the third function of the Connect Potential Operating System, thinking, is situated.

The lobes (sections) of our cortex map to the entire human body. The frontal lobe is responsible for higher-order cognitive processes and movement (thinking and action), the parietal lobe for processing sensory information, the temporal lobe for auditory processing and aspects of learning and memory, and the occipital lobe for visual processes. It is also where "words create worlds," because the cortex is where language lives. Your cortex constantly maps and re-maps your experience of the world, communicating with your limbic system where you consciously or, most often, unconsciously ascribe feeling to your experience. These thoughts and feelings impact the actions that you take. There is a constant train of thought running in this part of our operating system—again, most of it automatic and unconscious.

With your hand brain in the light fist, look at the knuckles just above your fingernails, because these represent a part of the above-your-ears brain that is critical to connecting potential, the pre-frontal cortex. This region, sometimes referred to as the executive center of the brain, brings together the functions of the cortex (thinking), the limbic system (feeling), and the brain stem (action), allowing us to make complex decisions, regulate our behavior, and interact effectively with the world—or, in my language, connect our potential.

PUTTING IT ALL TOGETHER

At this point in our discovery journey, I remind you that what I have paraphrased is an oversimplification of what actually happens moment by moment in our whole human brains—it does not nor is it intended to capture the intricacies, complexities, or nuances of this amazing system. If I have piqued your curiosity or deeper clarity is required, I invite you to dive into the sources cited at the end of the book and on the Community Hub. I encourage you to wait until the end of the book because I have taken an oversimplification approach on purpose so that this theory is sticky and can be easily applied into useful teachings and practices that I share throughout the rest of the book.

Think of the Connect Potential Operating System as a rigid minimal structure—rigid enough to give it foundation and clear parameters, and minimal enough to allow for flex and flow—a container to hold and organize your learning and more importantly the actions you will take as a result. So, to recap:

- Your Connect Potential Operating System has three main functions (aligned with Dr. Siegel's hand model of the brain):
  - o   Action (brain stem)
  - o   Feeling (limbic)
  - o   Thinking (cortex)

Now that you are familiar with the elements of the system, our next step is to explore how it operates when in one of two states: connected or disconnected. When it's connected, you can act, feel, and think with energy, ease, and effectiveness. When it's disconnected, you often act, feel, and think in states of strain, swirl, or stuck.

CONNECTED OPERATING SYSTEM =
Energy, Ease, and Effectiveness

DISCONNECTED OPERATING SYSTEM =
Strain, Swirl, or Stuck

Let's experience this using your hand model of the brain. Last time, I promise! Pick up your hand and hold it in a "connected" state (thumb tucked in, cortex fingers curled over—all parts connected). Now imagine for a moment that you are told by an authority figure something like, "You have a personality defect" (remember that zinger?), or you are cut off in traffic, at the end of a busy day where you had no time for lunch. Your amygdala is hijacked, and your reaction is to do what Dr. Siegel calls "flip your lid" by flipping your four fingers upward, disconnecting them from your other hand-brain parts. When was a time recently that you "flipped your lid" and had the experience of disconnection? I know that you have some to draw from because we all do living with the challenges of a VUCA world (reminder—volatile, uncertain, complex, ambiguous). I call them "good" and "not so good" moments. Let's dive deeper into each of the three functions of our Connect Potential Operating Systems and then put them together in the experiences of both "good" and "not so good" moments—connection and disconnection. In doing so, you can really understand and experience the need for the practices that keep it connected again and again.

ACTION—THE REALM OF INNER AND OUTWARD IMPACT

Action is a critical part of the Connect Potential Operating System. Without it no potential is ever connected, and we are just left with interesting thoughts and inspiring feelings that go no further. Dr. Huberman asserts that our action and behavior is the most important aspect to our nervous system: "the only thing that creates fossil records of our existence." So critical, he reports, that 70 percent of our nervous system functioning goes into it. That insight definitely gave me pause. How about you?

As I get into the Connect Potential Core Practice in this section of the book, I will teach you about the specific importance of action and physical movement for all parts of our operating system and how to incorporate it at strategic times when you most need it to connect potential. For now, I will take us away from the literal physical aspects of action into the language of action and how what we do with it leads to tangible impact. Let's start with a short visualization.

Take a moment to **see** a new red car. Now see yourself **getting into** that car. **Smell** the leather and the "new car smell." **See** yourself **driving** the red car along a coastline. Maybe the top is down and you **feel** the wind **blowing** through your hair. Now **stop** and **park** the car at a viewpoint, **get out**, and **take in** the magnificent view of the majestic rock formations and pounding waves. **Notice** that you suddenly **jump back** as a clap of thunder **jars** you out of your reverie and you **dash** back to the red car to **avoid being soaked** by the sudden rainstorm (remember to **put the top back up** if you put it down!). Now **come back** to the book.

What turned this red car from an object into a rich visual and visceral experience? It was the use of verbs, or action words. Verbs, a grammar device, are the language of action in the brain, making the pictures we see turn into dynamic experiences in our inner worlds. And actions are how we turn our thoughts and feelings into something tangible in the outer world. Let's look at how this works and why it matters.

We don't only use verbs to describe the physical experience that I walked you through in the previous visualization. We use physical language—action language—to describe our thinking and feeling experiences as well.

- "I am *struggling* with this problem." (You likely aren't physically in a struggle with the problem although it may feel that way)

- "My heart is *bursting* with pride." (That would be messy if it actually did!)

- "I am *overwhelmed* by emails." (I am certain that the emails aren't physically throwing themselves on you en masse through your computer or phone right now)

- "We will *reach* new heights together." (I assume that you aren't on a mountain, in an airplane, or climbing a ladder together)

- "I can't *grasp* your concept." (I hope that isn't your experience in this moment!)

The above examples are intended to help you see that the action function within your operating systems connects not only to your physical worlds but your mental (thinking) and emotional (feeling) ones as well. And the actions that you see internally lead to actions that you do externally. These actions result in experiences and outcomes that either move you closer to where you want to be with energy, ease, and effectiveness or further away with strain, swirl, or stuck. Feelings are the connecting point between your actions and your thinking, so let's explore those next.

FEELING—THE REALM OF ENERGY IN MOTION

Emotion: "energy in motion" or "e-motion." I don't remember the first time that I thought or said that phrase, but I do remember the first time it had a noticeable impact on a leadership team I was working with. The team was designing a set of agreements, their team's "working alliance," and one of the members proposed that the team take emotion out of their decision making and only use data and logic. At that point I paused the conversation and switched gears with the following two questions. Question one: "On a scale of one to ten, how important is your health to you?" The responses from the group ranged from eight to ten. Question two: "On a scale of one to ten, how would you rate your current health habits?" Not surprisingly, the responses to this question were lower, ranging from a three to a six, and accompanied by uncomfortable laughter as the group realized that logic doesn't drive our decision making and accompanying actions as much as they thought it did; emotions do. Everyone in the room agreed that it wasn't lack of knowledge that caused the gap between what they said was important and the decisions and actions they took; it was their emotions. And these emotions—energy in motion—determined the action that we would take or not take.

While the leaders in this example and you as well know that exercise gives us energy and is good for us, we often don't get up and do it because we feel too tired, stressed, or overwhelmed. If logic truly drove our health behaviors, many of us would eat less, exercise more, get more sleep, and drink more water instead of coffee. We have gotten really good at rationalizing our emotional decisions with logic after the fact—"I was too busy to exercise today"—so we don't notice what is actually driving what. After this part of the conversation, the leadership team agreed that using data and logic was still important to inform their decision making and agreed to be cognizant of the team emotions, addressing them rather than attempting to eliminate them.

Dr. John Kotter, one of the thought leaders in change management, also supports the notion that emotions matter through his work and research on what leads to change. His original supposition was that change happens as follows—through logical thinking:

- o We gather information
- o We analyze and think through the information
- o We act (change) based on our analysis

While it is inaccurate to say that logic doesn't matter at all—it does—what Kotter found to be of more impact was this:

- o We see something (in the world or in our thoughts)
- o We feel something (emotion)
- o We act (change) based on our emotions

Again, if what I just shared isn't entirely clear or resonating in your thinking, let's experience the power of emotions and the feeling part of our operating system here with the short reflection below (now would be a good time to grab your journal!):

- o Think about a messy problem that you are facing—it may involve a difficult task, situation, or person. Imagine yourself in that situation where it is causing you strain, swirl, or stuck. Now ask yourself the following three questions:

  - What am I thinking, seeing, and saying to myself? (Remember, the brain thinks in pictures and communicates in words)

  - What emotion or emotions am I feeling as a result?

  - What action or actions do I want to take because of that?

Here is an example that comes up for me a lot. Often when I teach concepts like this, my participants will say, "Oh yeah, these are the soft skills." While that might sound quite reasonable to you, the phrase "soft skills" is triggering to me, resulting in the emotion of anger. I see myself not being taken seriously for the important work I teach because there is nothing "soft" about committing to safety practices, professionalism, or treating others with respect—and there is nothing soft about the action I want to take as a result! So if it is useful, go back to those three questions with another tricky problem and see what emotions come up for you and then shake it off. Remember that we carry stress with us long after the triggering stressor is gone.

Come back to that tricky problem again and this time think of it instead as a situation that has the potential for great learning and ask yourself the same three questions. I will share my example first because your answers may not come as quickly this time.

1. What am I seeing and thinking now?

   I see myself pausing when I notice I am triggered,
   and I remember that "soft skills" is a common
   term that isn't meant to be a slight.

2. What emotions am I feeling as a result?

   I feel a bit excited because we now have a teachable moment.

3. What actions do I take because of that?

   I smile and say, "Soft skills is a common term used that
   doesn't capture the importance of what they are. How
   many of you think it important to be professional and
   treat others with respect? Nothing soft about that,
   right? Instead, I encourage you to think of these as core
   skills because they are core to being a great leader."

Now it's your turn to reframe your tricky situation into a learning opportunity. Ask yourself the three questions and notice how your experience of it is different from the first time. I hope that you can see and more importantly have experienced how emotions are activated by our thoughts and then lead to action. Let's complete this chapter by looking at the power of your thinking.

THINKING—THE REALM OF WORDS AND WORLDS

Descartes's quote, "I think, therefore I am," captures the power of your thinking. For me, it speaks to the power of your brain's cortex, not only in its function of thinking, but in connecting your thinking to your identity—your "beingness" in your experience of the world, and your mindset in it. If you think, "I am a problem," you create a very different experience compared to thinking, "I have potential." It all is held in your thoughts.

So what is a thought? A thought may simply be described as the words that we tell ourselves consciously or unconsciously to create or "make up" the worlds that we live in—remember, "words create worlds." Rick Tamlyn, a seasoned coach and educator, is quoted as saying, "It's all made up." That is, every experience we have in this world, have had, or will have is influenced by our thinking. Dr. Peter Jensen (PhD, Sports Psychology), who has worked extensively with athletes through eight Olympics and corporate leaders across the globe, agrees that it's all made up; even time is made up. If this statement sounds a bit too out there for you, consider this teaching from Dr. Jensen for a moment: "One minute is very different depending on what side of the bathroom door you are on." I think that we all have experience as to the truth of this statement!

And our thinking gives us the ability to time travel—yes, travel through time—creating worlds and the part we play in them that are past, present, and future. Thoughts may be in the form of memories (past worlds), imaginations (future worlds), or the present moment (our now world). The past, future, and present ability of our thinking is a defining factor in human capacity and is significant to our ability to create, understand, and decide.

The thinking that I just shared might have your operating system spinning right now, so let's make it a real experience. Go to your journal and respond to these prompts:

1. One thing I've learned from *Potential: How to Connect What's Already There for Exponential Impact* so far is...

2. As a result of my learning I am going to... (Be specific on what you will say and do so that you can see yourself doing it)

3. What I notice about my experience of reading this book right now is...

If the answer to the last prompt wasn't, "Wow, I can really time travel with my thoughts!" think about this again. In remembering your learning, you went backward in time to something that already happened. In imagining what you might apply from your learning, you went into the future. And finally, by asking yourself what you are thinking now, you came back to the present moment.

Pretty amazing, all this time travel in just a few moments. And it is likely that you not only saw the world that you were in, but you saw yourself (your identity) in it—"I think, therefore I am." This is just one of the powers of our thinking and our thoughts. They are also instrumental in us having a problem or potential mindset and are powerful disconnectors or connectors of our operating system, particularly when you consider how they evoke the feelings that lead to our actions.

Let's next explore the experience of our operating system as a whole when it becomes disconnected resulting in the states of strain, swirl, or stuck and when it is connected and in the states of energy, ease and effectiveness. It's our final exploration before I share the simple yet powerful core practice that connects it!

POTENTIAL

ONE Mindset Shift

**From *Problem* to *Potential*,
grounding in what matters**

ONE Operating System

ACT, FEEL, THINK

Disconnected Operating System =
Strain, Swirl, Stuck

Connected Operating System =
Energy, Ease, Effectiveness

ONE Core Practice

THREE Dimensions of Exponential Impact

Within us as individuals
Between us in our relationships and teams
Around us in the cultures we co-create and contribute to

CHAPTER FIVE

Connected vs. Disconnected Operating System

A DISCONNECTED OPERATING SYSTEM—STRAIN, SWIRL, STUCK

Take a moment and think back to a day, a situation, or a moment where you, as Dr. Siegel describes, "flipped your lid," weren't your best self. A time when your operating system—your thinking, feeling, and action—was disconnected, resulting in an experience of strain, swirl, or stuck. You likely have one that comes to mind and may be unsure how to describe it. I will further elaborate on each of the three Ss so that you can more clearly identify what type of problem state you were in, because being clear on our experiences is important to move through them as you will see once we dive into the Connect Potential Core Practice.

> **Strain**
>
> *n.* a force or influence that stretches, pulls, or puts pressure on something, sometimes causing damage
>
> *v.* to exert (oneself, one's senses, etc.) to the utmost
>
> That feeling of being worn, held back, and being constrained from what you want to achieve or the experience you want to have. Instead of feeling ease you feel tension, and moving forward feels painful.

Through COVID, I was fortunate that my client work continued. It also gave me the opportunity to connect my potential in becoming more technologically savvy. While I was able to extend my reach and impact across time zones and the globe from my home office, a constant source of strain for me was effectively facilitating group dynamics through Zoom and Teams. By the end of each day, my eyes were exhausted from toggling from one participant tile to another. (I called it the Brady Bunch Syndrome—look up "Brady Bunch opening tiles" and you will see what I mean.) I was growing increasingly frustrated from having to work with groups this way and was clearly in a problem mindset. My operating system's experience looked and sounded something like this:

- "This doesn't work as well as face-to-face." (Thinking)

- "This is so frustrating!" (Feeling)

- "I am just going to give up trying to make it better and just get through these sessions until we can be face-to-face again." (Action)

In the example above, you can see how my operating system (thinking, feeling, action) had me in a place of strain. Strain that literally resulted in headaches at the end of several days. Other common experiences that result in the state of strain include things like:

- Completing yet another fifty-plus-hour week and still having an overloaded inbox and task list—and being too exhausted to deal with it.

- Dealing with the same problem or problems—over and over and over again—and having them turn literally into pains in your neck.

- Believing that you what you are doing won't make a difference and doing it anyway—all the while feeling like your energy is going nowhere.

Our operating system's experience of strain is much like when we strain a muscle on a run or in the gym—we can still move forward, but it is hard, and it hurts. And when I say *hurt*, I mean this both figuratively and literally because pain is pain in the brain whether is it physical or emotional. Under MRI scans, similar parts of the brain light up regardless of its source. And continuous strain takes its toll on us, leading to burnout with significant physical, mental, and emotional consequences.

I imagine just reading about these common strain experiences and impacts is creating some strain for you because of the pictures that come into your mind (remember, the brain thinks in pictures and communicates in words). Like we did earlier, let's shake strain off so that we can move into the next *S* state, swirl.

> **Swirl**
>
> *n.* a spinning mass or motion; busy movement or activity
>
> *v.* move quickly with a twisting, circular movement, or to make something do this
>
> That feeling where you are so busy that your head wants to spin off your body. Where while there is so much going on, there is nothing getting done, leaving you exhausted and having a hard time even catching a breath.

Before we jump into swirl, I want you pause for a moment and write down the word "busy" in your journal. If you want to simply "write" it in your brain for now, that will work as well. Now that you have the word busy in front of you, I would like you to circle and then...CROSS IT OUT. CROSS IT OUT. CROSS IT OUT. Why did I have you cross out the word *busy*? And why did I shout this instruction to you in all caps? And do it three times? It is because I want you to eliminate the word *busy* from your vocabulary. Let me tell you a short story to illustrate why.

In 2014, I was driving to present at an Executive Leader Team (ELT) meeting. I was sharing the plan for our upcoming Leadership Summit that I was responsible to design, prepare leader presenters, and facilitate. It was mid-January in Calgary, Canada, and yes, the stereotype was true on this day—it was snowy and cold. And as usual, I didn't leave enough time to account for the weather. My thoughts were swirling as I was driving, much like the snow outside. Would the meeting go well? Was I prepared enough? Would the ELT buy in to the different approach I was proposing? Then it happened. The light turned yellow, and the guy in front of me had the audacity to stop for it!

My swirl went to rage, my operating system disconnected, and I flipped my lid! How could this jerk stop when I clearly planned on running the light to be on time for the meeting?! My swirling thoughts picked up velocity and increased in intensity. *Oh great! Now I won't have time to review my notes! I am going to look like a fool! How could that traffic light not know how* busy *I am?!*

Then it hit me. *Busy* is a state of mind—nothing more. You see, I was sitting in my car in the middle of a snowstorm, not moving, not engaging with anyone, not getting anything done, and yet I was "busy." The result? My mind was swirling, my pulse racing, palms sweating, and my emotions out of control. (Remember that our thoughts, feelings, and actions are all connected.) Thankfully the light stayed red long enough for me to have this blinding flash of the obvious and not race ahead to my meeting in a disconnected state. In that moment, I had the powerful insight that being busy is simply a state of mind. And what happened after that? Once my blood pressure resumed to normal and I put my lid back on, I decided to eliminate the word *busy* from my vocabulary for one year and see how my world might change—because, that's right, words create worlds! Oh, and while the ELT didn't buy in to all my ideas for the summit, they adopted some while appreciating the insight and energy that I put into the plan.

My experiment of getting rid of the word *busy* revealed a lot over that first year. First, I realized how often we use the word *busy* in conversations. *"How are you?" "Oh, I am so busy,"* (a response that isn't even heard because the asker is too busy to pause and listen). *"How are you? You must be so busy,"* (without even waiting for a response before making the statement).

Second, I realized with *busy* comes status, importance, and perhaps even our worth. We often equate our value with how fast we are moving, how many things we have happening, and how quickly our mind is swirling. No matter that we aren't accomplishing anything— at least we are busy. And finally, I understood how busy begets busy. We are wired with nerve cells called mirror neurons, named "mirror" because they allow us to pick up and mirror what we are experiencing with others. When we encounter "busy others" it often creates a "busy self," creating an even greater tornado-like swirl each time it picks up someone else into its vortex. Those that don't get caught up in the swirl often feel cast aside as they attempt to connect with us and we are too busy to notice. In our unconscious attempt to feel worthy by being busy, we may inadvertently be letting others know that that they are not worthy in the process.

If any of this feels familiar to you, you are not alone. One pandemic that is not likely go to away any time soon? The "busy" pandemic affecting us all directly or indirectly, leaving us in a swirl that often goes nowhere or at least not where we most want it to go. And it can end up in situations and outcomes like this:

- You are running in a million directions, doing a million things, and yet getting nothing done! (Action)

- There are too many options—and you don't know which one will lead to the best decision, so you keep bouncing between them. (Thinking)

- You wake up at three in the morning feeling anxious with a swirling, busy mind, not even noticing that you are laying there in the dark with nothing going on around you! (Feeling)

If any of this sounds familiar, don't worry. The antidote is coming soon. But first let's pause and take a deep exhale to slow down the swirl before we look at the third *S*, stuck.

> **Stuck**
>
> *Adj.* unable to move, or set in a particular position, place, or way of thinking
>
> That feeling of not being able to move, of being rooted in somewhere you don't want to be, of wanting to move forward, yet not moving or getting any traction..

Think about a time when you were stuck. While you knew there was action to be taken, you just couldn't make a move. Even when we are in the state of stuck, with no outward action happening, there is a lot going on inside, like the following:

o You really want something, but just don't have the motivation or initiative to make it happen. (Feeling)

o You talk yourself out of acting with excuses and "yeah buts" that are both inside and outside of you—"yeah, but I did that before and it didn't work; yeah, but it won't make a difference if no one else buys in; yeah, but the answer will be no because we don't have the resources." (Thinking)

o You worry, over-think, and are plagued with indecision. (Feeling, thinking, and inaction)

That was me in 2017 when I first realized that I really wanted to start my own facilitation, coaching, and consulting practice. While I loved WestJet and being a WestJetter, I had a sense of dissatisfaction that there was more that I could do—the need to connect my potential in a different way. Despite this I found myself coming up with reason upon reason not to make a move while at the same time becoming increasingly dissatisfied with where I was and where I was (or wasn't) going.

It started to show up in my work, my leadership, my interaction with colleagues, and in particular with my husband. He kept telling me I needed to make a move, and I kept providing reasons why not—it wasn't the right time, I needed to finish my graduate degree in leadership first—in doing so further attaching myself more fully to the thing that I no longer wanted and distancing myself from what I did want because at the core I was afraid. I was afraid that I wouldn't get clients, wouldn't be successful, and wouldn't know who I was in work if I wasn't part of an organization and a group of people who I respected and admired. I often told colleagues who were amid transitioning their roles that everything has a season, and you don't want to stay past your best-before date. Yet I wasn't taking my own wise counsel, and it was having impact. While I felt the situation was pulling me down, I was the one keeping myself stuck. I would flip back and forth with my indecisiveness each time digging more firmly in place.

You can become stuck in a variety of ways and in many different situations. A relationship that no longer serves you, unhealthy habits that are holding you back, dysfunctional team dynamics that aren't working yet their familiarity means we stick with them. And my personal favorite, another month of renewing your streaming service even though last month was to be the last binge before opening a good book instead—the list goes on. In all these situations, repeating tapes of inner dialogue keep you from moving forward toward what you really want or seeing situations for what they really are, leaving you stuck. And even though it sucks, you stay where you are. Let's not stay stuck. Instead let's quickly review the three *S*s before moving into the three *E*s.

THE EXPERIENCE OF STRAIN, SWIRL, AND STUCK

While there are many ways that a problem mindset can manifest itself, the states of strain, swirl, and stuck are the three that I have found show up most often. When each shows up, it is a clear signal that we are in a problem mindset and our operating systems are in a state of disconnection between our thoughts, feeling, and action resulting in:

- STRAIN: I CAN MOVE, BUT IT IS HARD AND IT HURTS.

- SWIRL: I CAN'T STOP BUT I AM GETTING NOWHERE.

- STUCK: I CAN'T MOVE.

Take a moment to ask yourself how strain, swirl, or stuck show up for you. Is there one that is more a part of your problem mindset and pattern than others? Do they all vie for your attention and take turns getting in the way? Or is your experience a unique combination of two or all of them? Notice it now and then shake it off. Let's move now from the experiences of strain, swirl, and stuck to the three *Es* of energy, ease, and effectiveness.

A CONNECTED OPERATING SYSTEM—ENERGY, EASE, EFFECTIVENESS

Think of a time, a day, a moment where you were "you at your best"; you felt connected and were connecting your potential with energy, ease, and effectiveness, the three *Es*. I encourage you to write about this experience in your journal to further bring it to life. What did it feel like? What was happening around you? How did it change your view of the world? Like we did with the three *Ss*, let's go through the experience of each of these one at a time.

Energy

> *n.* the strength and vitality required for sustained physical or mental activity.
>
> That feeling of vigor and vitality—a spark, force or power that moves in and through us, resulting in us having the dynamic experience of being animated and alive, moving us forward and inviting others to do the same.

As stated in the definition above, energy is vital to connect potential, and energy also results from connecting it. Much like my frame for the word *potential* in this book is a so-called "positive" one, energy in the context of the three *E*s is also the kind of energy we want to have. While it is an intangible force, we can see it, hear it, feel it—and know it's there—and I believe that you can feel the energy in and behind the words that I share with you. It is also the *e* in emotion, giving us energy to move forward, and it is a powerful force both for and from the act of connecting potential. In short, it is a good thing that keeps us "going and going," much like the Energizer Bunny.

While the state of strain feels like working hard at the cost of our energy when our operating system is disconnected, when it is connected, our energy changes dramatically. While I shared earlier about the strain I experienced facilitating groups virtually during the pandemic, there's more to the story. An experience that I had with a global virtual learning group was the spark I needed to shift my operating system from disconnection to connection around online facilitation. While there were peaks and valleys in my energy as this mode of working stretched from six weeks, into six months, one year, and then two years, the potential that was connected from that initial spark continued to fuel my operating system through it all.

It was May of 2020, and I was completing my ORSC coaching certification (Organization and Relationship Systems Coaching). One of the requirements of this program was to complete a "world work" project by putting into action something that we were passionate about that related to coaching relationship systems (such as partnerships, teams, and cultures). My plan was to explore the power of coming together in community through the practice of yoga. But when March 2020 happened and yoga classes were temporarily suspended, this was no longer possible, and I identified another project.

While I was experiencing strain in the online facilitation I was doing, I was still curious about how it might be possible to create a different experience with it. So I made it my world work project and put out a call to colleagues around the world who might be interested in exploring the "potential of connection" through a virtual learning group. We had a small group of ten who shared this curiosity from across Canada, the U.S., and Europe, and the learning we co-created over the six-week program completely shifted my problem mindset into a potential one, resulting in the following experience in my connected operating system:

- o "Oh! It is possible to form strong connection and build a powerful community in a virtual way." (Thinking)

- o "I leave each session with more energy than I came in with." (Feeling)

- o "I dive into each session with a solid plan and flex it as the community shifts." (Action)

The potential that we connected within ourselves and between us was the energy and the catalyst for deep learning and impact in ways none of us could have imagined, and the connections that were formed through this community live on in various forms today. I can't say that every group I worked with after this one resulted in the same uplifting and empowering energy. I will say, however, that I came to appreciate the power of virtual connection and leverage it for impactful outcomes with groups across the globe in ways that were not possible before this experience. And while I love the energy that I experience every time I work with groups face-to-face, and it has a different quality than the virtual experience, I am confident in the effectiveness of both and more skillful at connecting the potential that exists in both mediums.

Let's move from my story to take a moment to reflect on and experience one of yours. Think about a time when you were in a potential mindset and your operating system was connected and in an energy state. Grab your journal and answer the following questions about that experience:

- What were you thinking because of this energy? What words describe your thinking? (e.g., clear, focused, imaginative, logical)

- What were you feeling? What were the different emotions? (e.g., energized, uplifted, confident)

- What actions did you take because of your energetic thinking and feeling? What was the impact?

To complete this discussion of energy, it is important to point out that along with energy comes effort, so unlike the Energizer Bunny, we don't keep "going and going…" nor is it desirable to do so. Unplugging and having a break, getting rest, and taking a breath is important. I know that I have had a good energy cycle when it's the end of a full day or week and my husband asks me, "You have been working really hard—how are you?" and I say, "I am tired, but it's a good tired and I am ready to relax." Speaking of relax, let's look next at the state of ease.

> ### Ease
>
> *V.* lessen, release or relax
>
> *Adv.* freedom from stress or anxiety
>
> That feeling of being unencumbered, moving with fluidity, flow and freedom, where we experience progress without undue effort and things feel simple.

After the energy of the last section, let's pause for a moment and take a breath together. Take a deep, slow breath in through your nose, pause at the top of the inhale for a moment, then slowly exhale all your air out through your mouth—you might even want to let out an audible sigh. If that felt good, do it two or three more times and then come back to the words. If you feel a little bit dizzy, don't worry. Your deep breaths have just given you a boost of oxygen that, if not your regular practice, may feel a bit strange. From this place of relaxed breathing, let's further explore the experience of ease in our operating systems.

Ease is the root of the word *easy*, yet I don't think that *easy* captures what it means in the context of connecting potential. Ease is much more than the simple momentary punching of a red "that was easy" button. Ease is an experience that we can have through the entirety of our experience—even when it's challenging—when we have a potential mindset. So instead of *easy*, I use the word *easeful* because the experience is full of ease. So once again, just breathe in and out and feel yourself become easeful in this moment.

Earlier in this chapter, I shared the start of the "eliminate the word *busy*" experiment and what I learned right away—how much we use the word, how the word is like a status symbol or badge of honor, and how busy begets busy, creating busy swirls in us, between us, and around us. What I will share now is what happened as the year-long experiment continued and what shifted when the word *busy* was no longer part of my vocabulary—eliminating the problem mindset and swirl state it created.

Almost immediately after I decided to consciously eliminate the word *busy* from my life, someone came up to me at work and said, "Pam, I know you are really busy. I have a quick question for you—do you have a minute." My immediate hardwired reaction was to say, "You're right—I am busy! Go away!" Instead, I did this:

- I paused to notice the mindset and state that the word *busy* triggered in me. (problem swirl)

- I took a complete breath—inhaled and exhaled.

- I placed myself in the present moment and said, "There is a lot going on. I have a moment right now. What's your question?"

Those three steps—"pause, breathe, place"—took less than ten seconds, and it was the reset that I needed to get out of *busy* and into the present moment with my colleague. Because remember, *busy* is simply a state of mind—one that when left unchecked triggers a problem mindset resulting in the state of swirl. This simple yet powerful practice—"pause, breathe, place"—is one that over many, many repetitions became my hardwired go-to for ease in the moment and one that I have since taught to thousands of people wanting to escape the busy swirl and experience more easefulness.

Over the year of my "busy" experiment, I also found over time that not only did I experience more ease in every moment, but I got way more done because I wasn't wasting my energy with my busy mind. The truth is there is always a lot going on because, remember, we are in a VUCA world (volatile, uncertain, complex, and ambiguous). That is why I use the prompt phrase, "There is a lot going on. I have a moment right now," because it both acknowledges this reality while placing me in the present moment.

So to recap, to eliminate the word *busy*, practice this:

- ☐ **PAUSE** AND NOTICE.
- ☐ **BREATHE** IN AND **BREATHE** OUT.
- ☐ **PLACE** YOURSELF IN THE PRESENT MOMENT ("THERE IS A LOT GOING ON. I HAVE A MOMENT RIGHT NOW.").

A critical element in the *place* step is the phrase "I have a moment right now," because it prompts you to be in the present moment. If you don't follow "there is a lot going on" with it, you have just turned *busy* into more words.

Let's take time now for a short reflection and easeful moment. Grab your journal if it's nearby. First, breathe in and breathe out. Then take a moment to think about a time when you experienced ease—where you were relaxed, present, and ready in the moment. Breathe in and breathe out again.

- What were you thinking because of this ease? What words describe your thinking?

- What were you feeling? What were the different emotions?

- What actions did you take because of your easeful thinking and feeling? What was the impact?

So far in our exploration of energy, ease, and effectiveness, we have sparked with energy and relaxed with ease. Let's move now to the third *E*: effectiveness.

> ### Effectiveness
>
> *n.* the degree to which something is successful in producing a desired result; success.
>
> That feeling of getting it done and done well, achieving success, intended results—being in a state to get it done, do great work, and have positive impact.

Before we explore effectiveness, I would like you to go to a mirror, look into it, and with conviction say the following words to yourself: "You are a control freak." Repeat: "You are a control freak." Go do it. I'll wait.

I first experienced this exercise with Dr. Henry Cloud, an international bestselling author, speaker, leadership expert, and clinical psychologist. In this activity that I have repeated with hundreds of groups we turn to a partner and at the same time say these words to each other. You may want to do the same with colleagues in the office or on a Zoom meeting, or at home with your family right now—or maybe not, because context is everything. The point of this activity is that we are all control freaks to some extent. We have the need for control because control equals safety in our operating systems. When we believe that we are in control, we feel more certain, and when we feel more certain, we feel safer. Our perceived lack of control is one of the things that often keeps us stuck and gets in the ways of our effectiveness.

And there are lots of things we don't control, including the actions of others and often the outcomes we desire. So, while the effectiveness definition that I shared at the start of this section may imply that it is all about outcomes, it is not—although successful outcomes are more likely the result when effectiveness is the experience in your operating system. Effectiveness is more about your being and doing rather than having (outcome).

When we are in an effective state, we are motivated to act despite the things that we don't control because we are focused on what we can control, which is ourselves and our state (our being) and we are clear and decisive about our next action (our doing). These descriptors are the opposite of the state of being stuck—unmotivated, full of excuses, unclear, and indecisive. So how might effectiveness be experienced in our operating systems? I next will share how it looked in mine as I shifted from stuck to effective in making my move from WestJet to start my performance practice, Connecting Potential.

Leaving WestJet was the most difficult decision of my career. I was working with a group of people who I loved, respected, and admired, and connecting potential within, between, and around me. I was also in a senior leadership role that was both challenging and rewarding, two key ingredients for this potential connector. In the role I had the opportunity to work with and influence the culture across WestJet as I worked with all levels and all teams as the director of culture activation. I was in love with my job and the people that made my work so meaningful. And yet the season was complete. So, what moved me from "stuckness" to effectiveness, and what was the impact?

It started with two simple statements that I said out loud to myself and those closest to me, "It is time for me to move on. And leaving is a process." These simple statements, that were not so simple to say in the first place, marked the turning point to move me from a problem to a potential mindset and a stuck state to an effective one. Once I said those words, the following happened in my operating system:

- I was motivated to take the next step because the pressure for it all to happen now was off. (Feeling)

- I started telling myself that every action I took was one step to both move myself forward *and* to leave my organization in a better place through the process. (Thinking)

- I committed to taking one action each day to move in the direction I wanted to go. (Action)

- I gave myself permission to feel all the tough feelings that came with leaving an organization I worked at and loved for fourteen years. (Feeling)

- I celebrated each forward movement with an internal and sometimes external "high five." (Action)

Obviously, there was much more that happened along the way. My path to leaving, while set in a forward direction, was not a straight one. My intention in this story is to show you how effectiveness is mostly about the state of your operating system—your thinking, feeling, and action—and when you take control of those things, you move forward more effectively.

Once again, I invite you to think about a time when you and your operating system were in a state of effectiveness. When you took control of your being and doing, and your having came because of that. Where you had your intended impact and got your desired outcome. And even if you didn't, the experience was a good one because you did your best. In your journal, reflect on these questions:

- ☐ What were you thinking because of this effectiveness? What words describe your thinking?

- ☐ What were you feeling? What were the different emotions?

- ☐ What actions did you take because of your thinking and feeling? What was the impact?

Finish off by giving yourself an internal high five because you were effective, and we need to celebrate progress much more often than we do!

THE EXPERIENCE OF ENERGY, EASE, AND EFFECTIVENESS

When you are in a potential mindset and the three parts of your operating system—thoughts, feelings, and actions—are connected, your energy, ease, and effectiveness also connect and build on each other resulting in an overall experience like this:

- ENERGY: I HAVE ENERGY TO MOVE, AND EACH MOVE ENERGIZES ME!

- EASE: I AM RELAXED AND FULL OF EASE.

- EFFECTIVENESS: I AM EFFECTIVE, AND MY ACTIONS LEAD TO THE OUTCOMES I DESIRE.

One final thought on our operating system and its two states of disconnection and connection before we move into the core practice that connects it. We are always in one state or the other (disconnected or connected), often moving between them throughout the day, the week, or the month. If you find yourself in a problem mindset and the states of strain, swirl, and stuck right now, please don't despair or "should" on yourself. It is part of the human journey that we all experience time and time again. The key is to know that your operating system is disconnected, get clear on what you want instead, and then make the move toward where you want to be. Easier said than done, I know! So how can you actually make it a reality? This is what we get into next with the Connect Potential Core Practice. Let's jump into the practice that keeps your operating system connected and primed to connect potential within, between, and around you.

POTENTIAL

**From *Problem* to *Potential*,
grounding in what matters**

ONE Operating System

ACT, FEEL, THINK

Disconnected Operating System =
Strain, Swirl, Stuck

Connected Operating System =
Energy, Ease, Effectiveness

- **Strain:** I can move, but it is hard and it hurts.
- **Swirl:** I can't stop but I am getting nowhere.
- **Stuck:** I can't move.

- **Energy:** I have energy to move; each move energizes me!
- **Ease:** I am relaxed and full of ease.
- **Effectiveness:** My actions lead to the outcomes I desire.

ONE Core Practice

THREE Dimensions of Exponential Impact

Within us as individuals
Between us in our relationships and teams
Around us in the cultures we co-create and contribute to

CHAPTER SIX

The Connect Potential Core Practice

As you know from your lived experience, moving from one day to the next can be overwhelming amidst *busy* work and *busy* lives. What?! did I just use the word *not* to be used? I did to make a point. While I think that I have made a compelling argument for the value of committing yourself to connecting potential, I also appreciate how challenging it can be—no, *is*—to meet the demands of each day without having to think about one more thing. So as enticing as this notion of connecting potential may be as you sit in this place and perspective of curious reader, it is something that can feel quite elusive as you get caught up in the noise of work and life—noise both around you and the loudest noise most often within you.

Let's cut through the noise with a core three-part (remember that three is the magic number) practice to connect potential that I call the Connect Potential Core Practice—shocking, I know. This practice is profound in its simplicity and its impact. Because while the world and its challenges are complicated and complex, connecting potential amidst challenges can be quite simple. So, I must ask you this powerful question (borrowed from one of my Brain Gym mentors) before we move on.

"Is it okay that this practice is simple for you?"

This question is both tongue in cheek and real and direct because while we say that we crave simplicity, we often make things much more complicated and complex than they need to be. We are going to take Einstein's advice of "make things as simple as possible here, but no simpler" as we move through the practice. So I will ask you one more time:

"Is it okay that this practice is simple for you?"

You said yes? That is wonderful because the practice I have created and am about to share with you comes from my synthesis of decades of learning, learning again, and layering new learning. Although each of the three practice elements are underpinned by a robust body of knowledge from disciplines of behavioral and neurosciences and informed by teaching and wisdom from contemplative traditions including yoga and meditation, the practice itself is simple—on purpose. While I will share useful background as I take you through it, I want this practice to become a core part of your routine so that you get the maximum benefit from it. For that to happen, it needs to be simple enough to include in a full day, full work, and full life yet effective enough to make the difference needed for you to connect potential and move forward through challenges big and small with greater energy, ease, and effectiveness.

It is also important to point out here that as I take you through the three parts, you will likely see elements that you already do—keep doing them! I have a number of practices that I have incorporated into my life and work. Why the Connect Potential Core Practice is my core go-to is because it is one that engages all three parts of our operating system (thinking, feeling, action), integrating our whole human brain along the way, and is designed to keep our Connect Potential Operating system, well, connected! Enough talking about the practice; let's get into and experience it—The Connect Potential Core Practice: Intend, Notice, Move.

THE CONNECT POTENTIAL CORE PRACTICE—INTEND, NOTICE, MOVE

At a high level, each of the three parts are this:

o Intend—set an intention for how and who you want to be
o Notice—take a pause and notice how and who you are now
o Move—take an action to move toward how and who you want to be

Let's look at (and more importantly experience) each of the three parts to begin hardwiring them into your practice and operating system.

INTEND

"Energy follows intention." (Hania Khuri-Trapper)

One of the things that I love about this quote is that right at the beginning of the practice, you are doing something that supports your energy, one of the goals of doing the practice in the first place. When you consciously set intention, you activate a part of the brain that lives in your thinking realm of your operating system, the cortex. While the workings of the brain in thought, intention, and consciousness are still largely hypothetical and not fully understood, researchers like Dr. John Medina, author of *Brain Rules*, provides insight into why intention so powerfully energizes our operating systems. His work explains how a portion of intention is housed in the parietal lobe, a part of the cortex that is responsible for sensation, movement, and perception, linking the thinking and action parts of our operating system. The moment we set an intention we move from a place of automatic, unconscious thought, feeling, and action to one where we are aware and conscious, directing energy away from the automatic parts of the brain (the brain stem and limbic system)—the feeling and acting realms of our operating systems—to the thinking one. This part of your operating system is the place where you can use your ability of time travel for a useful purpose—to look ahead and begin to create a reality that doesn't even need to have happened yet to be experienced as real. You decide how you want to be and there is power in that. Let's intend right now.

SETTING AN INTENTION

Think about how you want to be as you continue reading this chapter. Pause for a moment to complete this statement in your mind or better yet your journal, setting your intention:

- "To be _____"

See, nice and simple. My intention as your practice guide is to be clear and compelling as I teach you the Connect Potential Core Practice.

Let's up the ante on intention setting by thinking about a challenge you are currently facing. It might involve another person who might be frustrating you, a task that you have been avoiding like tracking your monthly expenses (or maybe I am the only one who does that), or "just" the words you are saying to yourself to keep you in a place of strain, swirl, or stuck. The words that create the most vivid worlds are often the ones we say to ourselves.

Once you have your challenge in mind, set an intention in your journal for how you want to be in that situation. For example:

> The words that create the most vivid worlds are often the ones we say to ourselves

- In the situation of the frustrating person:
    - o To be curious.
    - o I am patient.
    - o I listen with empathy.

- In the situation of the monthly expenses:
  - To be proactive.
  - I am clear as I complete them.
  - I enjoy doing my expenses. (Okay, maybe that one went too far.)

- In the situation of the words you tell yourself:
  - To be kind to myself.
  - I am committed to action.
  - I focus on what I control. (Remember we all are control freaks of some form or another.)

What you might have noticed in these examples is that I deviated from the formula "to be" and gave you two other ways to frame your intentions, "I am" and "I [verb]." While "to be" is a perfectly fine way to frame an intention, what I have found from doing this work with hundreds of potential connectors is that the more we can frame our intention as something that already is or an action that we can immediately take, the more powerful it is. "To be" is something that we want, "I am" is something that we are (even if only in our intention in that moment), and "I [verb]" puts action in our inward mind so we can more easefully demonstrate it outwardly. I will leave it to you to choose your intention starter—"to be," "I am," or "I [verb],"—as we move forward setting our intentions throughout the book.

POTENTIAL VS. PROBLEM FRAMING

It is also important to frame our intentions using "potential" language instead of "problem" language because each frame creates a very different experience in our operating systems—our thoughts, feelings, and actions. Neuroleadership expert Dr. David Rock discusses how "toward" and "away" responses in the brain and body create different conditions (or what I call states) because of the chemicals that are produced. Potential language sets the frame that this intention is something that we want to move toward. Problem language sets the frame that it is something we want to move away from.

When we frame an intention using potential language (something we want to move toward) it activates the production of "feel good" chemicals like dopamine (our reward chemical), endorphins (our pleasure chemical), serotonin (our happy chemical), and oxytocin (our connection chemical). These create conditions in our operating systems that lead to positive and productive thinking, feeling, and action. They can result in an opening in our thinking, a receptiveness in our feelings, and motivation in our action—connecting all three parts. This makes it more likely that our intention will become a reality.

When we frame an intention using problem language it results in a very different experience in our operating systems due to the chemicals associated with the stress "fight or flight" response namely, adrenaline and cortisol. Both stress chemicals result in disconnection in our operating system and, when strong, are enough for us to flip our lids. At the very least the parts of our operating system become disconnected from each other—our thoughts, our feelings, and our actions—and it is hard to move forward with energy, ease, and effectiveness. Instead we experience strain, swirl, or stuck.

Dr. Peter Jensen also paints a compelling picture of why it is important to state our intention from a potential "what we want" mindset with this paraphrased example.

> "Imagine asking someone to go to the grocery store to get groceries for dinner and giving them this instruction. 'Don't get chicken, don't get bread, and don't get peas.' What is the likelihood that they will come home with the ingredients you need for the dinner that you want to make? Not very likely!"

It is important that we set intention with a potential, "what we want" frame rather than what we don't want for our operating system to be primed for the next part of the practice and for us to have the clarity we need to move forward. Here are some examples of words and phrases to say (and not to say) when setting intention. As you read them, notice the experience that each creates in your operating system and how each one differs.

POTENTIAL-FRAMED INTENTIONS	PROBLEM-FRAMED INTENTIONS
▪ To be… I am… I [verb]	▪ Not be… I am not…
▪ Will	▪ Won't
▪ Start	▪ Stop
▪ Could	▪ Should
▪ Be energetic	▪ Be less tired
▪ I am calm	▪ I am not anxious
▪ I act with clarity and confidence	▪ I try to act with clarity and confidence

Now, please write down the word *try* in your journal (or in your brain). Much like with the word *busy*, I would like you to circle and CROSS IT OUT, CROSS IT OUT, CROSS IT OUT! Why did I have you add this to the list of words not to be used? Despite your initial thought, it is not because Yoda said, "Do or do not, there is no try"—although Yoda and his wise words are quite compelling. The reason is because the word *try* evokes stress in your operating systems and that is the last thing you need when setting an intention for how and who you want to be. It also gives you permission not to do it. Think about a time when you said, "I tried," and didn't really do anything. Let's do a quick experiment with two simple instructions:

1. Look up from this book and now look back at the page. Simple, right?

2. Now *try* and look up from this book and then *try* to look back at the page. How was this experience different?

It is likely that the first instruction resulted in you easefully looking up and looking back down, while the second instruction resulted in a hesitation and momentary tightening as your system asked itself, "Can I do this?" If this experiment did not result in a new insight for you on the stress created by the word *try*, think about a time when you were "trying really hard" or you said, "But I tried!" In either of those experiences were you able to access the energy, ease, and effectiveness that you desired to have? When my son was ten, he taught me a lesson about the word *try* that neither of us will ever forget.

It was Halloween night 2009, a big event in our household (my husband is the Clark Griswold of Halloween), and our boys were excited to go out and trick-or-treat. The only problem was that Halloween fell on a Sunday and our older son had a major project due that he left to the last minute. And why on earth would a teacher make an assignment due the day after Halloween?! I was not a parent who hovered over my children with their homework—partly because I wanted them to own the responsibility and partly because my brain was too tired at the end of a long day to help them, if I am being perfectly honest. My son let me know at three thirty that he had this project due the next day, and I let him know that it needed to be completed before he went out to get candy. He stomped down to the basement with these words: "Okay, I'll try!" When he came back upstairs an hour later, I wasn't sure what he had meant by *try*, because the project was a mess. While once again, I am a parent who believes that my children's homework should be their work, not mine, I couldn't let this one slip by. When I let my son know that trick or treating would have a hard stop at 8:00 p.m., and then he would have to go back to the project and do more work on it, you can imagine what his reaction was—it wasn't great.

Something he said really stuck in my mind, and it changed everything. He said, "But Mom, I tried!" And in that moment I saw that he had and saw the stress that his trying had created for him. So I said this: "Honey, I know you tried and I can see that you are frustrated. My question for you is did you do your best on this?" He looked down and muttered, "Not really." So I asked, "How important is it for you to do your best?" He looked up at me and said, "Important, but I'm trying and it's not working." And he was right! When you "try" and put yourself into a problem mindset, it is really hard to get your operating system working—at least with the energy, ease, and effectiveness that you have the potential for.

We agreed that he would go get candy and when he came back, he would take one hour to do his best with his project and see what happened. He got his candy, filled up on it, and with the sugar high and frame of "do his best," he did. Was it an amazing result? Not really. Did he feel good about it and the fact that he did his best? Absolutely. It was the last time that I recall him using the words "I'm trying." And with an intention of doing his best again and again, he has gone on to do amazing things. He is now the PhD student I referred to earlier in the book, and I am so proud of his continued commitment to excellence in learning.

So when might you be more intentional about where you direct your energy with Intend? How about:

✓ At the start of each day

✓ At the end of the day before rest (yes, rest, that thing that many of us don't do)

✓ Before an important conversation

✓ Before a team meeting

✓ As you take on a challenging task

✓ When you notice yourself in a problem mindset

This last point leads us to the second part of the Connect Potential Core Practice: Notice.

NOTICE

*"The range of what we think and do is limited
by what we fail to notice."* (R.D. Laing)

Let me take you back to January of 2014 and my epiphany about the word *busy*. I was in my car with not much going on as I sat at the red light. But I was "b*sy," and the longer I sat, the "b*sier" and more stressed, aggravated, and frustrated I became. The faster and more jumbled my thoughts were as I continued to "awfulize" what would happen next. (*Awfulize* is another gem from Dr. Peter Jensen.) My breathing was rapid, my palms sweating, and my jaw locked in tension. In fact, if the light turned green, I would likely have missed it as I was so deep into the experience of flipping my lid. And I would not have broken out of this swirl and had the teaching point of eliminating the word and all the benefits that came with that decision if not for one thing—I noticed my experience.

Notice is the second part of the Connect Potential Core Practice, right after Intend. Having said that, the skill of noticing is a power practice in and of itself, and it is one that I have worked to deepen through the practices of yoga, meditation, and Qigong, under the incredible mentorship of my teacher, Stephanie Nosco. Until we notice our experience—specifically the experience of our operating system—our thoughts, feelings, and actions—we cannot be at choice. That's right: until we notice our experience now, we cannot be at choice on how we move next. And here is why.

The thoughts, feelings, and actions of my racing heart that I described in my red light story were automatic reactions that resulted from the problem mindset I was in and they "just happened" due to my fight/flight reaction that was triggered in that moment. I didn't consciously tell my thoughts to swirl and jumble, feelings to become anxious, my jaw to tense, my palms to sweat, and my frustration to escalate—that just happened as an automatic reaction. Only when I noticed what was happening did the insight that "b*sy" is just a state of mind become my conscious thought, shifting my mindset from problem to potential, and my operating system experience from one that was unconscious and automatic to one that was conscious and intentional.

Noticing activates a similar part of the brain, the cortex, as intention does—in a sense placing it next to it. The act of noticing places us consciously in the present moment, and this is significant because the only place we can move forward from is where we are now. Let me repeat that—the only place you can move from is where you are now, and noticing places you in the now. It not only places you, it grounds you, giving you a foundation to move forward from. Let's take a moment to notice.

Wherever you are now, I want to you pause and notice your experience in the present moment. Specifically, I want you to check in with your operating system and ask yourself the following questions to check in with its three parts—thinking, feeling, and action. If you have it with you, feel free to respond in your journal to these prompts:

- What am I thinking?

  o What is the nature of my thoughts? (e.g., are they clear, muddled, moving slow, moving fast)

- What am I feeling?

  o What words best capture the emotions I am experiencing in this moment?

  o How strong are these feelings? 1 = barely registers, 10 = very strong

- What is "actioning" in my body? What physical sensations do I notice? (e.g., what areas of my body come to my attention, what is my breathing like, are there areas of tension)

You might notice now that you held your breath during this last noticing experience, because you are learning it and "trying" to do it right. There is no right way to notice, so exhale, go back to the start of the exercise, and do it again, this time breathing through it.

Because so many of us live our lives overly focused on the experience happening above our ears—our thinking—I want you now to go back to noticing the physical sensations in your body right now. If there is a place on your body where you particularly notice something, place your hand on that place. For example, as I write these words, I become aware that after yet another day of travel and a hotel room bed, I notice sensation in my upper back when I pause from typing to place my hand there. With your hand placed on the part of your body where you notice something, now ask yourself, *What is the word behind the hand?* This might sound like a strange question, and it might well be because we are so disconnected from our bodies in our b*sy thinking worlds. So go back, scan your body, place your hand where you notice sensation, breathe, and ask yourself the question again. The word behind my hand is *tired,* so I am going to pause on writing and take a short movement break. What is your word?

I am back and glad to speak with you again! I learned this "brain-body" noticing hack early on in my Brain Gym training, and it is one of the most powerful tools I share with my clients when they find themselves in the states of strain, swirl, or stuck in an "above your ears" way—where their above-your-ears brain is disconnected from their whole human one. Because remember that all parts of our whole human brains and the Connect Potential Operating System are connected (thinking, feeling, action), and the more we can notice all the parts of our experience, the more we bring all parts and resources of our operating system online.

Sometimes people don't like to notice because they intuitively know that what they uncover will be "negative," unpleasant, or uncomfortable. Please know this: it's *already happening*—once we notice it, we begin to move the energy from all the places in our operating system where it is already (often unconsciously) happening to the part of our system where we are conscious of it and where our intentions live. Only when we notice our experience can we be at choice about what to do with it and decide what action we want to take. I will say this again—noticing gives us choice and the potential for powerful decisions no matter what our noticing uncovers.

Throughout the book I have used two labels that I actually don't like to use, "negative" and "positive." Now I will share why, starting with these two questions for you: Have you ever had an experience that in the moment felt negative—only to have that experience be the thing that in retrospect was the best thing that could have happened to you? That you connected potential and grew in ways not despite that negative thing, but because of it? I will assume that your answer is yes, because we have all had those experiences—some small and some big. I shared one of my big ones as the learner with a "personality defect" at the beginning of this book. Was the experience awful, destructive, and hard? Absolutely. Was it an important part of my story that led me to where I am now? Yes! Was it so-called "negative"? Of course it was.

The problem with labeling something as negative is that it gets in the way of us connecting our potential. Using the label of negative puts us in a problem mindset without understanding what the experience is. It is a word that assesses and even judges our experience without describing where we are now. When we say something is "negative" we want to negate it, nullify, make it invalid. Our experiences in the now—all of them—are valid because they are what is happening now—and once again, the only place that we can move forward from is from where we are now. And when we label something as negative, it is like we put a period or exclamation point on it, not to be further explored or unpacked, in a sense closing our minds to it. And a closed mind is a hard place to learn and connect potential from. As uncomfortable as the experience of noticing where you are now can be, it is an essential element to *move* forward, the final part of the Connect Potential Core Practice that we will get to shortly. Finally, the act of noticing and naming our experience is also a powerful step to move from a problem mindset to a potential one. Dr. Siegel has coined the phrase "name it to tame it" because the act of naming so-called negative experiences and emotions, which requires us to notice them first, lessens the emotional charge and impact that that emotion has on our system. It is the reason that we use language like, "It feels good to get that off my chest," or, "I needed to vent," or we sigh and relax after we honestly name what we are experiencing in a difficult situation that triggers negative emotions. Note my use of the word *honestly*. When we say that we are "fine" when we clearly are not, the real emotions that we experience continue on with greater impact than if we named them honestly.

On the note of so-called "positive" experiences, the same thinking applies. Without getting clear on what makes that experience so, we are less likely to learn from it for future ones. And I also think that we have all had experiences where something felt "positive" in the moment, only to see afterward that in fact it didn't lead us where we wanted to go. I am writing these words as we are amid the holiday season. Those chocolates, treats, and extra helpings of stuffing might feel positive right now—but will feel negative in the New Year when I go put my work pants back on!

When are some key times to start the practice of noticing? They are the same as the ones for intending:

- ✓ At the start of each day
- ✓ At the end of the day before rest
- ✓ Before an important conversation
- ✓ Before a team meeting
- ✓ As you take on a challenging task
- ✓ When you notice yourself in a problem mindset

Remember that noticing involves noticing the experience of your whole operating system—thinking, feeling, actioning, so that you bring it all online to benefit from the third part of the Connect Potential Core practice: Move.

Before we move there, I think it helpful to share with you some noticing *dos* and *don'ts*:

NOTICING DOS	NOTICING DON'TS

• Describe what you are experiencing in all three parts of your Connect Potential Operating System:
 	
  o Thinking
 	
  o Feeling
 	
  o Actioning
 	
• Do the "place your hand on it and name the word behind the hand" for whole-system noticing
 	
• Remember to pause and breathe to really notice
	• Don't label your experience as positive or negative—it is just what you are experiencing now
	
	• Don't judge yourself for what your experience is—it is where you are now—it's already happening and because you have noticed, you are at choice to decide what to do next
	
	• Don't stress if you can't locate sensation in your body—remember many of us have hardwired ourselves to live above our ears—noticing that you don't notice is still noticing! Ta da!

I hope that I have convinced you of the importance of noticing and that you practice it often to hardwire it as a powerful habit that gives you choice to decide how to move next. Move is the third part of our Connect Potential Core Practice, which puts our intention into action. So let's move into it!

MOVE

"Movement is the doorway to learning"(Dr. Paul Dennison)

And movement is also the doorway to connecting potential. As I shared earlier in the book, the information and insights that inform the Connect Potential Core Practice come from my learning in diverse fields of behavioral science and neuroscience, contemplative practices like yoga and meditation, and they are grounded in years of professional and personal experience. This is particularly relevant with the third part of the practice—Move.

I want to you to imagine for a moment that I have just brought a newborn baby into the room and placed the baby in their bassinet beside you. Now imagine me saying the following:

> Okay baby, I want to you to lay there, still for the next five years. And while you are laying there not moving, you will develop the ability to go from seeing in black and white to color, you will be able to focus from seeing blurry images to ones that are clear in detail. You will also be able to discern the nuances of nonverbal communication and communicate nonverbally yourself—all while not moving. You will begin to understand that symbols put together into words and sentences have meaning and you will be able to put together sounds and symbols, at first incoherently, then coherently, as you develop the ability to communicate with words. While you won't do it right away, while you are laying there not moving, you will also develop pathways in your brain that form the basis for you in a few short years to start putting symbols called "letters" onto paper (I hope that we are still using paper and writing instruments when you have this conversation!) in ways that convey information and emotion. And later you will put together these things called numbers in your head to compute equations and formulas. All this will lead to you creating something that might not yet exist in your mind before

you create it in the world. And all of this will happen while you lay there not moving for the first five years of your life.

Ludicrous, right? We would never say or believe this! Early *movement* is essential for our cognitive functioning later on. We understand the power of movement not only for the physical skills we need in life but for our mental and emotional skills as well. Dr. Paul Dennison, the creator of Brain Gym, made it his life's study and work to develop the practice of using simple developmental movements to support our capacity to learn and move through learning challenges with energy, ease, and effectiveness. Sound familiar? Earlier in the book I shared that I have been a licensed Brain Gym instructor for over twenty years. This method and practice was instrumental in my mental health healing journey and is now a core part of how I facilitate my continuing connect potential evolution and help others do the same. It is a key part of the Connect Potential Core Practice and something that makes it unique as a performance practice in the space of individual, team, and organizational development. A participant at one of my keynote speaking events on potential exclaimed to me that I had successfully cracked the code and "corporatized *woo-woo!*" While there is nothing *woo-woo* about the connection between our action, feeling, and thinking, I appreciate her appreciation of me bringing it into the world of work and hope that you do too. And it is critical to connecting potential, whether we are two years old or forty years old.

And here is why. While we can all agree that movement is essential for infants and their cognitive development, we forget this as early as age five when we start telling children to sit still and stop fidgeting. We then wonder why they have difficulties in learning. As I write these words I have an image—somewhat exaggerated to make a point—of children sitting in their desks with straitjackets on trying to learn—think about the stress and barriers that this produces! However, this book is not about how the ways in which we teach children need to change—there are many great books on the topic referenced on the Community Hub.

As Dr. Dennison likes to put it, sitting is the new smoking. While perhaps not as bad for us as smoking, it is a far more common practice! We need to physically move throughout our lives, not just for our physical health, but for our thinking and feeling performance as well. Our operating systems are similar to computer ones in that when either of them sit inactive too long, they shut down and "go to sleep." While we may not physically fall asleep from long days sitting in front of screens, our operating system often does—resulting in lags in our thinking and feeling performance. So it is important to "jiggle our mouses" with movement every fifteen to thirty minutes.

What is true when you were two years old is still true now: movement is the doorway to learning and to connecting potential. Let's experience it with our most core and continuous movement, the act of breathing. Our breath is so important as a *move* tool to connect our potential that the rest of this chapter focuses on it—so breathe in and breathe out and let's do it.

BREATHING IS MOVING

Take a moment to notice your level of energy and focus right now and give it a number 1–10 (1 = barely registers, 10 = very high). Next identify the number that represents what your optimal energy level is; for me it is about an 8—high but not too high because then I begin to swirl.

Once you have noticed your energy level, we are going to do something that you are already doing and until now weren't conscious about—breathing. Our breath is our most potent movement tool because not only is it something that we do all the time, it is the one automatic body function that we can do both unconsciously *and* consciously. Randelle Lusk, yoga teacher, somatic coach, and creator of the Rare Method, beautifully describes the connecting power of conscious breath like this: "If you really allow your breath to be felt, to be deliberate, then your body will be reunited with your mind via your breath… because our mind holds our thoughts and our body our felt sensations." When we breathe consciously, it is a powerful regulator of our operating system and a catalyst to connecting our potential in the moment.

Start by simply noticing your breath and as you are breathing, ask these noticing questions:

- Do I breathe in through my nose or my mouth?
- Do I breathe out through my nose or my mouth?
- When I breathe, what moves first—my chest or my abdomen?
- Is my breath short or long? Shallow or deep?

An interesting thing happens when we notice our breathing—it changes and becomes longer and deeper. This is a simple example of how the act of noticing shifts things in the moment. Let's now consciously shift our breath by breathing in through our nose and out through our mouth three times:

1. Breathe in through your nose for a count of four and out through your mouth for a count of four.

2. Breathe in through your nose for a count of four and out through your mouth for a count of four.

3. And one more time—breathe in through your nose for a count of four and out through your mouth for four.

Then take a pause to notice what's shifting.
Finally, make these three moves:

1. Using a four-count in and out, breathe in through your nose so that your abdomen moves before your chest. You may want to place your free hand on it to draw attention to that area of your body.

2. Breathe out through your mouth, emptying your abdominal region first and emptying yourself of breath.

3. Repeat two more times—in through your nose and out through your mouth. In through your nose and out through your mouth, moving your abdomen with your breath.

Notice your level of energy now. What is the number now and how optimal is it in this moment? Because you were likely close to your optimal energy level when you started this experience, you might not have noticed too much of a shift, so let's amplify the experience by increasing your level of stress.

Think about a person, place, or thing that is causing you stress right now. It might be me for asking you to do all this breathing, and that is fine because it is for an important purpose! As you place yourself in this experience, notice what happens in your operating system. You might notice that your thoughts and feelings turn "negative" and that your body actions contract and tighten, remembering that they all impact each other. As you experience this situation of stress, ask yourself the following questions:

- What am I thinking?
  - What is the nature of my thoughts? (e.g., are they clear, muddled, moving slow, moving fast)

- What am I feeling?
  - What words best capture the emotions I am experiencing in this moment?
  - How strong are these feelings? 1 = barely registers, 10 = very strong

- What is "actioning" in my body?
  - What physical sensations do I notice? (e.g., what areas of my body come to my attention, what is my breathing like, are there areas of tension)
  - Place your hand where you notice sensation and answer this question: what's the word behind the hand?

Now take three breaths with me. You can stay with a four-count in and out, or extend it even longer.

1. Breathe in through your nose deeply so that your abdomen moves first and exhale fully through your mouth.

2. Breathe in through your nose and exhale through your mouth.

3. One last time, breathe in through your nose and exhale through your mouth, maybe even letting out a sigh.

Now go back to that challenging situation and notice what has shifted in your thinking, feeling, and action by asking these questions:

- What am I thinking now?

   o What is the nature of my thoughts? (e.g., are they clear, muddled, moving slow, moving fast)

   o How have they shifted?

- What am I feeling now?

   o What words best capture the emotions I am experiencing in this moment?

   o How strong are these feelings? 1 = barely registers, 10 = very strong

   o How have they shifted?

- What is "actioning" in my body now?

   o What physical sensations do I notice? (e.g., what areas of my body come to my attention, what is my breathing like)

   o How have they shifted?

   o Place your hand where you notice sensation and answer this question: what's the word behind the hand now?

It is likely that you feel more relaxed, your heart rate has slowed, and you also experience shifts in your thoughts and feelings. If not, take conscious breaths in and out until it does.

This is the power of our most core and continuous movement: our breath. "Simply powerful," to quote a fellow coach, Peter Hill. In the moment, the breath can shift us from a problem to potential mindset and our operating system from disconnected to connected. I will illustrate this by sharing a story that is very present for me because it happened as I was writing this part of the manuscript and then unpack what happened in two key paths of the nervous part of our operating system—sympathetic and parasympathetic.

My arrival into this part of my first draft manuscript coincided with a mindset retreat in Colorado Springs with my business coach, David Bayer. To say it was an incredible, integrating, and inspiring experience does not do it justice because in it, I got to a new level of releasing my hardwired pattern of pleasing, performing, and perfecting to connect potential and become more present and purposeful. Intuitively I knew that this experience would lead to a story in this book. Little did I know it would be the one that follows.

I departed the retreat on a Monday morning with an early wake-up of 6:00 a.m. I was tired, a "good tired," and looking forward to my flying time to get some writing in. I packed the night before and made sure that I had all my essential items together so that the early morning departure to the airport would be easeful.

I shared a car service with my wonderful colleagues, and the ride was filled with uplifting conversation and completed with hugs and well wishes. I got to the check-in agent, who asked me to present my passport, and when I went into my wallet to get it out of its pouch, it *wasn't there!* Immediately I flipped my lid, not only because it was missing and all that came with that, but because this was not the first time I'd had passport issues (I had one stolen at Gatwick Airport four years earlier), and I imagined the call of shame to my husband to say that it happened *yet again!*

In that moment my mouth went dry, my thoughts went wild, and I didn't know what to do. It was a unique combination of swirling while being stuck. I was throwing things out of my handbag and diving into my carry-on bag all while thinking, "Why the hell is the customer service agent just looking at me with such a blank stare?!" and, "What am I going to tell my husband and what will the Canadian passport office say to me?!" While there was a lot going on, there was really nothing productive happening because I was so disconnected.

Then I remembered—"just breathe"—so I began first by exhaling through my mouth because the panic caused me to literally hold my breath. It took a few exhale breaths before I even had room to take any breath in. While not fully connected, I was able to think, feel, and act because of those breaths in a more integrated way that looked something like this:

- "It may have dropped out in the car because I know I had it last night when I packed. I will text my colleague, who booked our driver, to get her contact info," (Think)

- Text colleague. (Act)

- "Remember to breathe in and breathe out." (Think, act)

- Ask the check-in agent how much time I have before I might miss my flight. (Act)

- Get the driver's cell number and call her to ask if she saw my passport. (Act)

- She hasn't, so more panic—exhale again. (Feel, act)

- Ask the driver if she could pick me up to take me back to the hotel, and she says yes! (Act)

- Remember to exhale. (Act)

- Call the hotel to ask them to check if my passport is there. (Thinking ahead and taking action)

- Remember to exhale. (Act)

- "There are worse things than being stuck in Colorado Springs with time to write." (Think)

- Start to calm down from the reframe of the experience. (Feel)

- Call the driver again to check on her ETA as she is pulling up to the curb. (Act)

- See that she has my passport in hand and let all the air out. (Act)

- Feel relief and gratitude and thank my driver. (Feel, act)

- Call the hotel to tell them that I have my passport so they don't need to send security to look for it and thank them for doing so. (Act)

- Continue on through my check-in experience with a smile and conscious knowing where my passport is throughout the process. (Think, feel, act)

- See my colleague, express my appreciation, and laugh over how this is a great story. (Think, feel, act)

- Realize that this story really makes the point about the power of the breath in real time and feel excited to share it. (Think, feel)

- Write this story as a timely teachable moment. (Act)

- Relax and enjoy the onboard snacks as I write. (Feel, act, think)

I hope that this story made it as real for you as it was for me, making the point that the simply powerful act of conscious breathing can shift your operating system from disconnection to connection.

It does so by moving your nervous system from a sympathetic to parasympathetic response. I'll finish this chapter by explaining what happened in my nervous system in both my problem and potential mindsets and how the breath was the key in moving me from one to the other. Again, as with all the technical information I am sharing with you, I am keeping it as simple as I can on purpose and have resources for you to dive into on the Community Hub.

Most simply put, our nervous system, which my mindfulness and yoga mentor Stephanie Nosco pointed out is designed to make us nervous, has two distinct parts and paths—the sympathetic and parasympathetic.

SYMPATHETIC—"FIGHT OR FLIGHT"

The sympathetic nervous system is mostly commonly associated with the automatic stress response of 'fight or flight' because when activated it gets us ready to act by releasing adrenaline and cortisol (stress hormones), increasing our heart rate, respiration, blood pressure, dilating our pupils, and slowing our digestive system.

These reactions to sympathetic activation are important for our ability to "fight or flee" and were very useful in the time in our evolution when the threats where primarily of a physical nature. Remember though that words create worlds in our operating systems and that most of the threats in modern times are of a psychological nature—yet the reaction of the sympathetic nervous system is the same.

Because humans can time travel in our minds, moving from past memories to future imaginations, we have the unique ability to hold onto the stressor even if it is no longer present or hasn't even occurred yet (and most often, doesn't even occur). This continued, chronic over-activation of the sympathetic nervous system is what we experience when we persist in a problem mindset, leading to strain, swirl, and stuck, and is why prolonged stress results in chronic illness because of the wear on our systems from our physiological reactions to it.

Another key contributing factor to the wear and tear of overactivation of the sympathetic nervous system reaction is that the system is designed to support action by readying us for physical movement—in other words, fight or flight. Do you know how long a sympathetic response is useful in our systems? Ninety seconds—yes, that's it, according to Dr. Dennison. Enough time to fight the predator or flee to safety thousands of years ago, or to react in an emergency if someone were to yell "fire" right now.

The sympathetic system is not all bad, though, because it gets us ready to act when action is useful. That feeling before an important meeting or writing an exam—nervous energy, dry mouth, butterflies in the stomach—those are all signals that the sympathetic nervous system is getting you ready to take action, and that is a good thing because action is needed.

The challenge is that this system is too often activated when the threats are made up in our mind and/or we don't do anything with the energy it creates by acting or moving. Or we don't get back into a parasympathetic response and recalibrate the system with what it is designed to do: help us relax, or commonly called "rest and digest."

I was in a sympathetic response throughout all my "passport panic" experience because I didn't really calm down until some time after I had tucked it safely into its compartment. By consciously moving my breath, however, I was able to regulate my sympathetic system in the moment so that I could feel, think, and take the action to resolve this problem. Let's explore next how the parasympathetic system works to help us relax so that we can get our operating system back into a place of integration and connection.

PARASYMPATHETIC—"REST AND DIGEST"

As already stated, the parasympathetic nervous system is commonly described as the "rest and digest" system. In my passport story, while I didn't pause for a nap or to have a snack, pausing to breathe began its activation, allowing me to somewhat relax my thinking, feeling, and action so that it was more intentional. In retrospect, I was also able to more effectively "digest" the experience to be able take intentional action. Let's look at how this system can get us from strain, stress, stuck to energy, ease, and effectiveness.

The parasympathetic nervous system is also automatic and responsible for many life-sustaining processes when your body is in a state of relaxation including your heart rate, blood pressure, and digestion.

It balances our sympathetic nervous system after times of stress or danger by relaxing and reducing our body's activities—slowing heart rate, respiration, and blood pressure, all conditions needed for clear, thoughtful responses.

The parasympathetic nervous system aids in digestion as it promotes the production of saliva and the motility or movement of food through our gastrointestinal tract. This is why we get a dry mouth and digestive upset when we are stressed and the sympathetic reaction overrides.

It also acts on the eyes to stimulate receptors in them and contract the pupils to help us see up close more clearly. It also activates tear production to keep our delicate eye tissue healthy. Metaphorically, it may also be why we can "see" what we could have done in a stressful situation after the fact when parasympathetic response has kicked in and we are relaxed.

While the experience of the parasympathetic nervous system is often not as acute as the sympathetic one getting us ready to act it is nonetheless critical to our ability to connect our potential, because it creates the conditions needed for easefulness while effectively managing our bodily systems.

Both the sympathetic and parasympathetic nervous systems play critical roles, and it is important to have the right system activated for the right purpose. I notice as I complete the descriptions of both that even the way we most commonly refer to them—"fight *or* flight," "rest *and* digest"—speaks to the aspect of disconnection (*or*) and connection (*and*) within our operating systems that each creates. I love when connections like that reveal themselves and hope that you do too!

The breath is an important activator of both systems. When we breathe in, we primarily activate the sympathetic nervous system that gets us ready to take action, and when we breathe out, we primarily activate the parasympathetic nervous system that lets us relax. And, because when it comes to connecting potential, we need to be both ready and relaxed, the next practice we are going to do together integrates the power of "words create worlds" and the breath for added impact.

I Am Ready and Relaxed

I was going to share this practice with you later in the book, but it is so simply powerful, I didn't want to wait. Here it goes:

> Breathe in and say to yourself, "I am ready."
>
> Breathe out and say to yourself, "I am relaxed."
>
> Breathe in "I am ready."
>
> Breathe out "I am relaxed."
>
> Breathe in "I am ready."
>
> Breathe out "I am relaxed."

It's that simple. I do this practice every day, often several times when the pressure is on, to regulate and recalibrate my operating system, and no one even knows I am doing it except for the energetic, easeful, and effective way that I show up after.

To recap, each part of the Connect Potential Core Practice—Intend, Notice, Move—has an important function and impact:

o   **INTEND** ORIENTS OUR OPERATING SYSTEM TO WHO AND HOW WE WANT TO BE.

o   **NOTICE** ALLOWS US TO BECOME AT CHOICE FOR OUR NEXT MOVE.

o   **MOVE** IS THE DOORWAY TO CONNECTING OUR POTENTIAL WITH OUR BREATH AS OUR MOST SIMPLY POWERFUL TOOL.

ALIGNING IS MOVING

I'll share one more movement exercise to close this chapter. Seated where you are, take a moment to notice your core. Now notice how your spine facilitates the movement of your core. First gently rock side to side, moving laterally left to right. Next rotate your spine toward the left and then to the right. Finally, slowly tuck your chin and curl forward and then extend back up, mimicking the yoga action of "cat" and "cow." Not only did you just give yourself a nice body-brain break, jiggling your mouse, you also experienced the critical importance of alignment. When your spine is aligned, you can move in all six directions with energy, ease, and effectiveness. Now imagine for a moment that your back "just went out" and your spine is misaligned. Notice the difference in your movement experience and how it is no longer energetic, or easeful, or effective. Notice any discomfort or pain and where your focus goes. That's right—it goes to the pain point rather than how you want to move.

Alignment matters emotionally and mentally as well as physically. Think about a time when you were asked to do something that was out of alignment with your values. What was that like? Or a time when you were part of team that was misaligned. How did that get in the way of your work together? Or finally when you had the experience where an organization said they valued one thing and then repeatedly did the opposite? How disengaging was that? When there is alignment, we can move forward with energy, ease, and effectiveness in all dimensions and with all parts of our operating system connected. When there isn't—we cannot. In the stories to come, you will see how alignment is key to moving forward in a connected way.

> When there is alignment, we can move forward with energy, ease, and effectiveness in all dimensions and with all parts of our operating system connected. When there isn't—we cannot.

Next let's put Intend, Notice, Move together as one practice so that you can understand and experience how the "whole is greater than the sum of its parts" for even greater impact. Take a breath and let's go!

POTENTIAL

ONE Mindset Shift

**From *Problem* to *Potential*,
grounding in what matters**

ONE Operating System

ACT, FEEL, THINK

Disconnected Operating System =
Strain, Swirl, Stuck

- **Strain:** I can move, but it is hard and it hurts.
- **Swirl:** I can't stop but I am getting nowhere.
- **Stuck:** I can't move.

Connected Operating System =
Energy, Ease, Effectiveness

- **Energy:** I have energy to move; each move energizes me!
- **Ease:** I am relaxed and full of ease.
- **Effectiveness:** My actions lead to the outcomes I desire.

ONE Core Practice

INTEND, NOTICE, MOVE

THREE Dimensions of Exponential Impact

Within us as individuals
Between us in our relationships and teams
Around us in the cultures we co-create and contribute to

CHAPTER SEVEN

Putting the
Practice Together

Several years ago, I was part of a learning and development team working on our team effectiveness through a facilitated development session, where we practiced what we preached and were the clients, not the facilitators. The conversation became quite heated because we were all stressed from high workloads and competing demands and priorities from the business. At some points in the conversation we were strained, at others swirling in circles, only then to find ourselves stuck. There may have been a few lids flipped in the process as well. We decided that we needed a longer lunch break for each of us to recalibrate. I was sitting at my desk catching up on a mountain of email—not how I recommend you take a break to recalibrate—and one of my team members stopped in front of my cube looking quite distressed. My quick question to her was "Do you need some Brain Gym?" To which she quickly replied, "Yes, please!" I had previously taken her through an introduction to the method (movement to shift brain wiring) and she appreciated its benefits. We didn't have time for a full five-step Brain Gym Balance, so in the moment I put together a shorter practice that I am now teaching you—Intend, Notice, Move. We ducked into a meeting room where I had her:

- Intend how she wanted to be with the team (open and receptive),

- Notice how she was in the moment (anxious, frustrated, not wanting to participate in the afternoon conversations), and

- Move using the power of three breaths and continuing with PACE, a core Brain Gym power practice that I share on the Community Hub.

After going through the practice, she was ready to participate with an open mind. We completed it by celebrating the shift before getting back to work, because we don't celebrate progress near enough! Throughout our afternoon conversations my colleague was a constructive contributor, with her energy helping to change the dynamic of the team to a more productive one. At the end of the session, she thanked me for taking her through a practice that, while simple, was profound in its impact. One year later, she participated in Brain Gym 101, the introductory twenty-four-hour course to this powerful method, and she has used the tools and practices with her colleagues and clients to this day. Since that day, Intend, Notice, and Move has been my go-to approach to connect potential with everyone I work with, becoming the core practice I will take you through now. Once again, I am grateful for the problem because it was the catalyst to connect this potential.

To start, I would again like you to think of a situation, a challenge, a continuing problem where you are experiencing strain, swirl, or stuck and would like to experience greater energy, ease, and effectiveness. As I have done throughout the book, I am going to do the practice with you and share my experience along the way. This would be a great time to grab your journal to take notes as we move through it together!

CONNECT POTENTIAL CORE PRACTICE: INTEND, NOTICE, MOVE

Intend

What is your intention for the experience that you have just identified? More specifically, how do you want to be in it? Create your intention by completing one of the following statements. Choose the statement starter that resonates most with you:

1. To be...

2. I am...

3. I [verb]...

You can write this intention in your journal, on a post-it note, or in your mind. You may even want to say it out loud to engage the auditory part of your operating system in the process. Below are some examples to help prime the intend part of your operating system:

-   To be present... I am present... I pay attention

-   To be curious... I am curious... I listen with curiosity

-   To be energized... I am energized... I bring energy

Remember to have your intention framed as something that you want, rather than something that you don't want, to start you in a potential rather than problem mindset.

Example of my intention: **To be both clear and concise in taking you through this practice.** Both are important because I am not physically with you to see where you need clarification throughout it.

Notice

Once you have your intention set, we move into the next part of the practice—notice. Place yourself back into the situation where you are currently experiencing strain, swirl, or stuck and notice your current experience. It will be one that is different than what you intend. If it aligns with your intention—great!—setting intention was all you needed to shift from problem to potential. For the purpose of experiencing the complete practice, ask yourself, what would disconnect you from your intention in this situation? I am asking you to perturbate yourself on purpose so that you can experience the power of noticing and movement. Yes, *perturbate* is a real word that means to disrupt and agitate because this is the place where learning starts!

Let's go back to noticing your current experience. As you see yourself disconnected from your intention, instead experiencing strain, swirl, or stuck or some other uncomfortable state, ask yourself the following noticing questions:

- What am I thinking?
    - o What is the nature of my thoughts? (e.g., are they clear, muddled, moving slow, moving fast)

- What am I feeling?
    - o What words best capture the emotions I am experiencing in this moment?
    - o How strong are these feelings? (1 = barely registers, 10 = very strong)

- What is "actioning" in my body?
    - o What physical sensations do I notice? (e.g., what areas of my body come to my attention, what is my breathing like, are there areas of tension)

- Place your hand on your body where you notice sensation and ask:
    - o What's the word behind the hand?

Example of my noticing:

- My thoughts are running faster than my words making it hard to stay clear and concise. (Thinking)
- I am a bit anxious and unsure. (Feeling)
- I keep stopping and getting stuck on where to go next in explaining this to you. (Action)
- My hand went to the left side of my neck and the word there was "tight."

Now that you have noticed, there is likely some tension or discomfort between where you are now and where you want to be—exactly where you need to be at this part of the practice. For example, for me it is not easeful to move forward in a clear and concise way when I am "running, anxious, unsure, getting stuck, and tight"—an interesting combo of swirl and stuck. How about for you?

Move

We have our intentions and we have noticed where we are. So now let's literally move toward where and who we want to be with the two breath practices that we have already done and adding in one more.

First let's just breathe together. Become aware of your breath—its depth and whether it is more through your nose or mouth. Breathe in through your nose and exhale through your mouth so that your abdomen moves first on both the inhale and exhale. Deep abdominal breathing also activates the parasympathetic response. Repeat two more times, in through your nose and out through your mouth.

Then let's do the "Ready and Relaxed" breath three times together:

Breathe in and say to yourself "I am ready."

Breathe out and say to yourself "I am relaxed."

Breathe in "I am ready."

Breathe out "I am relaxed."

Breathe in "I am ready."

Breathe out "I am relaxed."

Finally, let's finish with three rounds of a technique called "box breathing." This technique is used by Navy SEALs, so it is designed to recalibrate us no matter how significant our sympathetic response is.

Breathe in for four counts.

Hold your breath for four (keeping your abdomen relaxed).

Breathe out for four.

Hold for four.

Breathe in for four.

Hold your breath for four (keeping your abdomen relaxed).

Breathe out for four.

Hold for four.

Breathe in for four.

Hold your breath for four (keeping your abdomen relaxed).

Breathe out for four.

Relax and return to your regular breath pattern.

Now that you have moved through the three breath practices, I want you to go back to the situation you placed yourself in for this practice and re-notice where you are now and what shifted.

Re-notice:

- What are your thoughts now? How have they shifted?
- What are your feelings now? How have they shifted?
- What is actioning in your body now? How has it shifted?
- Place your hand where you experience sensation now. What is the word behind the hand now?

Example of my re-noticing:

- I notice that my thoughts are clearer and more in synch with my typing fingers. I can get to the point easefully.
- My feelings are both calm and confident—I got this, and so do you!

- My actions—well, you are reading it—a clear and concise practice that helps you connect your potential.

Anchor in your intention:

Come back to your intention and state where you are now by completing this statement:

- I am...

It may be that you now are what you intended at the beginning of the practice—in my case, clear and concise—or you may have ended up somewhere else, for example:

Example of where I am now—my intention in action:

"I am clear on what I want this experience to be for my readers and excited to share it with you!"

That is the Connect Potential Core Practice—simply powerful and something that can be done anywhere, any time you want to get your operating system more connected. Take a moment and celebrate your progress and make a mental note for yourself of anything that we did that you really liked—that is your home "play" after this chapter because while the Connect Potential Core Practice works, it doesn't feel like work.

I use this practice with clients one-on-one and in small and large groups. And yes, I use it in a variety of corporate settings. The vast majority of the thousands of people I have done it with experience a shift, and a small number do not. If you didn't experience a shift, here are the common reasons why. Your intention was not as clear as it could be, or it was set with problem language (for example, to be less frustrated). You might be new to noticing your experience (particularly the actioning in your body) as many of us spend so much time focusing above our ears. Having said that, if you notice you didn't notice, that is noticing! Stick with it and you will build your noticing muscle. Finally, if the act of conscious breathing is new to you, it might feel awkward at first. Just keep breathing consciously, and it will become your go-to tool to move from disconnection to connection.

While there are benefits to each part of the Connect Potential Core Practice—Intend, Notice, Move—when done together they have even greater impact in our operating systems, and here's why:

Intend draws us forward.

Notice grounds us to take the first step.

Move gets us from where we are to where we want to go.

Let's unpack these statements further. We started with Intend because "energy follows intention." When we set our intention, we focused our attention on what we wanted, drawing it away from the experience of what we don't want—our problem. In our operating system this activated our thinking part. As a reminder, this is the part of our operating system that gives us the gift of "time travel" where we can start to see ourselves in a future state even though it's not yet happening. Remembering that "words create worlds," we started to imagine a new context, a new state, and in doing so began to shift the other parts of our operating system, our feeling and action, because if we can see it in our mind, we can feel it and action it. If we can't think it, we can't feel it or act it. Seeing it on the inside is the first step in making it real on the outside. Our intentions drew us forward, which was critical to connect our potential because our potential is never behind us. Let that one sink in for a moment—our potential is never behind us. This is the power of Intend—the first step in moving us forward and connecting potential.

> Our potential is never behind us

It was important to follow the first step, Intend, with the second step, Notice, because while this practice is about us moving forward with greater energy, ease, and effectiveness, we can only move forward from where we are *now*—no matter what the *now* is or how strained, swirling, or stuck the experience is. While our thinking and feeling parts of our operating system can time travel, the part of our system that acts—our body—cannot, at least not at the time of me writing this book.

Noticing our *now* also moves our unconscious experience of what's happening in all parts of our operating system closer to where our intention resides in our thinking part of the system. This is not intended to be a technically precise statement of what is specifically happening in your neurology—but rather a description of the experience that noticing offers us. We know that the conscious awareness of *now*, our noticing, lives in the thinking part of our operating system, as does our conscious awareness of what we want, our intention. So the act of noticing places our current experience with our desired one, creating the necessary contrast and tension to energize and prompt us to move. Dr. Peter Senge teaches and has coined this dynamic "creative tension."

CREATIVE TENSION—THE KEY DYNAMIC WITHIN INTEND, NOTICE, AND MOVE

Let's now look at why the dynamic of creative tension is critical to the Connect Potential Core Practice by revisiting our earlier process, with creative tension now integrated.

Intend draws us forward.

Notice grounds us to take the first step.

The creative tension between **Intend** *and* **Notice** *gives us energy to move, and* **Move** *gets us from where we are to where we want to go.*

In his book *The Fifth Discipline: The Art & Practice of the Learning Organization*, Peter Senge teaches about the dynamic of creative tension. This was one of the stickiest concepts for me during my graduate studies in leadership because it so clearly captured that dynamic—the tension between how we want to be (intend) and how we are now (notice)—that is needed for potential to be connected. And it goes like this.

Creative tension exists in the gap between what we want, envision, aspire to—what we Intend—and real and deep understanding of our current reality—what we Notice. This gap and the accompanying uncertainty create tension—*creative tension*—which is the necessary catalyst, impetus for us to Move. Dr. Senge uses the metaphor of the rubber band to teach this dynamic and I will take you through it now.

Imagine that you have a rubber band between your two hands or two fingers. If you have one, you might want to pick it up and place it around your thumb, representing the now, and forefinger, representing the desired future, of your non-book-holding hand. Once again, on the forefinger end of the rubber band is what you intend, or your desired future. On the thumb end is the way you notice you are being now, or where you are in relationship to your desired future.

Imagine for a moment in your mind or experience physically with the rubber band that you have an intention for the future but no noticing of the here and now by placing it around just your forefinger. That rubber band is just hanging off the forefinger, floating off on its own with nothing to ground it for forward action. Now imagine or take that rubber band off your forefinger and just have it around your thumb. You are now just grounded in the here and now with nothing pulling you forward into your desired future. To summarize:

Intention without Noticing =
floating ideas without impetus to move

Noticing without Intention =
nothing to draw us forward

Now play with the tension that lives between your thumb and forefinger either in your mind or with your hand and notice that the further apart they are, the more tension that is created with the rubber band. Not enough distance between them or not enough tension—there is no energy to move. Too much distance between them and the tension is too much, breaking the rubber band. So, while we want to have intentions that stretch us, we want the tension to be "just right"—much like in the fairy tale of Goldilocks and the Three Bears.

Also, while this creative tension is a powerful dynamic to energize forward movement, it can be framed in a way that does not achieve this goal—that is, what Dr. Senge describes as emotional tension. We know from experience that tension is uncomfortable—whether that is physical tension, emotional tension, or thinking tension. As human beings we want to avoid tension because it is uncomfortable and takes energy to hold it. As I write this, I just flashed back to the "wall sits" we used to have to do in gym class—remember those—sitting against a wall in an imaginary chair for a period that was probably seconds but felt like hours? If you didn't have that experience, move over to a wall with your book in hand and give it a go. Or don't, because you get to choose your experience in reading this book!

Once again, we like to avoid tension. When we don't see it as being a creative force it just makes us emotionally uncomfortable, so we back away from our intention rather than move toward it because even though our here and now may be unsatisfactory, it is certainty, making it the safer choice. Just think three words: "New Year's Resolution." How many of us have disappointed ourselves because we give up on resolutions we make on January 1st before January 8th? When I worked in the fitness industry, we always knew that our full gyms on January 2nd would have lots of space long before the end of the month. I am sure that you can relate to the experience of backing off what you intend because it becomes uncomfortable, and it might look like the following:

- Falling back from your New Year's resolution or goals for fitness and nutrition

- Letting ad hoc meetings land on your "thinking space" blocks in your calendar even though you know the thinking time makes you more effective

- Not following through on your development plan goals because you're just too "b*sy"

- Not having the tough conversations with a colleague even though you have committed to being courageous and having them in a recent team building session

The other choice that we can make is to use the energy created from this tension to move forward toward our intention. Just as moving the rubber band back toward your thumb (here and now) lessens tension, moving your thumb toward your forefinger (intention) does the same. Tension is lessened and the outcome is completely different where we move forward toward what we want, creating a new reality and connecting our potential in doing so.

In writing this book, a key milestone was getting draft one of the manuscript complete, and this required me to "just write," or "shovel sand into the sandbox." The sandbox method was one of the amazing processes that our coach Ashley Mansour taught us in the Author Accelerator program that she took us through. As I share in the acknowledgments section of this book, without this program, Ashley, and the sandbox method, you would not be reading it. And did it ever result in creative tension! You see, in the sandbox method it is critical to just keep shoveling sand into the sandbox—that is, get words on the page. To do this and get version one of the manuscript complete means no going back, no revisions, and no editing, not at all something that is comfortable for this pleaser, performer, and perfecter! I chose to lessen my tension by "shoveling sand" and getting words on the page even when I wanted to stop and edit, and completed my manuscript before the deadline. Now, I invite you to take a moment and anchor in how the experience of holding creative tension in your operating system has had a powerful positive impact for you as well. Think about a time when you held the tension between your desired future (intend) and your here and now (notice), turning it into a creative force that energized you to move forward and remember:

- Your intention of what you wanted to achieve (you may not have had it as clearly and consciously articulated as you do right now)

- Where you were at when you determined this was where you wanted to go—notice what were you thinking, feeling, and actioning

- The creative tension and energy—the gap created between what you wanted and where you were

- What it was like when you acted and moved to where you wanted to be—the feeling of accomplishment you felt when you got there. You might have not even experienced the sense of accomplishment when you did, so do that now. It is important that you anchor in this moment because it helps you "hardwire" the thinking, feeling, and action of progress and success as a resource you can come back to for future challenges.

Now take a moment to appreciate the power of the creative tension that happens between what you Intend and what you Notice. Because in the journey of connecting potential in a world full of problems, it will happen again and again, guaranteed. This creative tension creates the conditions for the third part of the practice to have its most powerful impact—so let's Move there next.

Move is the part of the Connect Potential Core Practice where our more inner and intangible actions of intending and noticing become both outer and tangible through action and movement. When we move our whole body, we use all the resources of our operating system, not just the ones that are above your ears. Think about a time when you were strained, swirling, or stuck around a tricky problem or situation, where you kept "trying" to come to a solution or resolution and you could not. You then "gave up," took a break, went for a walk with your dog, a workout, or just took a moment to breathe, and then suddenly you had an insight or a fresh perspective that allowed you to move through and resolve it—or at least get closer to resolution.

The power of movement, when we leverage it as part of a conscious practice and connect it to both our intention and noticing, is that it becomes the way to move forward all parts of our operating system—our thoughts, our feelings, and our actions—with greater energy, ease, and effectiveness. We have already activated our conscious, higher-order-thinking part of our operating system with Intend. Then we brought conscious knowing of our current experience to the forefront alongside it with Notice. While both are important to bring us closer to connecting our potential in the moment, it is not until we Move and bring our whole self into the practice that the shifts we are after become actualized, real, and tangible. Remember the powerful shifts that came with just three breaths. Movement is how we calibrate our operating system to align with what we have placed into it with our intentions and noticing. And ultimately it is what makes our inward experience manifest in outward action. When we bring our body into our best thinking and feeling we bring about our best thinking and feeling.

Once again:

> **Intend** draws us forward.

> **Notice** grounds us to take the first step.

> The **creative tension** between the two gives us energy to move, and

> **Move** gets us from where we are to where we want to go.

And the result is that we connect our potential in that moment and create energy, ease, and effectiveness!

PRACTICE MAKES...

Before we move into how you can apply the Connect Potential Core Practice even further, I would like you to complete this statement: "Practice makes _____." Was your first answer "perfect"? Did you start to think, "Hmmm...I bet this question is not as straightforward as it seems. Maybe she is after an answer like *progress* or *proficient*." All of those are good thoughts, and all of them are wrong because "practice makes *permanent*." I bet that as you read these words, you can think about a bad habit that you are really good at because you practice it over and over again! To benefit from a practice like the Connect Potential one, you need to consciously practice it to hardwire it and make it a habit. And here is why.

Imagine for a moment that you are in Canada in the late winter. There has just been a dump of heavy wet snow. Now imagine that you get to work right after this snowfall and need to walk from your car to your workplace through this fresh, heavy snow—that is up past your knees. Keep going because there is an important point to this. Now experience in your mind what this walk through the heavy snow is like and how much effort it takes to make the pathway from your car door to the building door. This is what it is like in our operating systems when we lay down the neural pathways of new learning and attempt to build new habits from them. It takes effort and energy, much like walking through that snow.

Next see that it is the end of the day (whew!) and several people have walked the pathway that you laid out in the morning, and because safety matters the pathway has been sanded and salted to prevent slips and falls. Imagine now how easy it is to take that pathway back to your car because it has been walked through over and over and over. This same experience happens in our operating systems the more we practice a thought, a feeling, an action. Through a process called myelination, our neural pathways become stronger and faster, making it easy to both access and use them.

Finally imagine now that I am directing parking out in the lot and close off that well-practiced pathway and tell you that you need to create a new one to get to your car. I imagine that your immediate reaction is "no!" because you like the one you already made. It is easier and forging a new path is too much work. Herein lies the challenge of shifting from habits that keep us in strain, swirl, and stuck even when we don't like the experience they produce, and creating new habits that result in energy, ease, and effectiveness. And much like the best workout programs we might be given in the gym, these practices only work when you do them. We only build new muscles by working them, and at first it will feel uncomfortable and take energy. And yet we know that when we stick with our workouts, the results are worth it.

One of the challenges of the Connect Potential Core Practice being so simple is that we forget to do it! So here is how I recommend you start hardwiring new pathways and habits by doing the reps. Do it three times a day for seven days and then repeat for two more weeks.

- In the morning before you begin your day:
    o Intend—what is your intention for the day? How do you want to be?
    o Notice—what are your thoughts, feelings, and actioning in the body as you start the day?
    o Move—the practice of three breaths.

- One time during the day before an important activity or conversation:
    o Intend—how do you want to be in that activity or conversation?
    o Notice—how is your thinking, feeling, and actioning now?
    o Move—the practice of three breaths.

- Before you go to bed at night:
    o Intend—how do you want to be as you complete your day and go into rest?
    o Notice—how ready your thoughts, feelings and actioning in the body are for sleep.
    o Move—the practice of three breaths (*not* while watching Netflix or doing email in bed!).

Want to really get the most out of the Connect Potential Core Practice? Well, there's an essential "bonus" step that makes it even more transformative that you have already experienced. At the end of each practice, *re*-notice how your state has shifted and come to your intention. This act of re-noticing and reconnection with your intention will help anchor you in the new present moment.

I hope that you can see and more importantly have experienced how putting together Intend, Notice, Move as a simple practice leads to powerful impact. On the Community Hub you will find a practice tracker to help you solidify this new way of being and doing.

Now, remember the three dimensions of potential? Within you as an individual, between you and your relationships and teams, and around you in the cultures that you are part of? Next we're going to dive into how our core practice of Intend, Notice, Move works in these dimensions.

Before we do that, pause, take a moment and a breath. Remind yourself why connecting potential matters to you and thank yourself for committing to doing it. If you are with me right now, you are connecting it—it's already happening. Let's keep going together!

POTENTIAL

ONE Mindset Shift

**From *Problem* to *Potential*,
grounding in what matters**

ONE Operating System

ACT, FEEL, THINK

Disconnected Operating System = *Strain, Swirl, Stuck*	*Connected Operating System =* *Energy, Ease, Effectiveness*
• **Strain:** I can move, but it is hard and it hurts. • **Swirl:** I can't stop but I am getting nowhere. • **Stuck:** I can't move.	• **Energy:** I have energy to move; each move energizes me! • **Ease:** I am relaxed and full of ease. • **Effectiveness:** My actions lead to the outcomes I desire.

ONE Core Practice

INTEND, NOTICE, MOVE

Intend draws us forward.
Notice grounds us to take the first step.
The **creative tension** between the two gives us energy to move,
Move gets us from where we are to where we want to go.

THREE Dimensions of Exponential Impact

Within us as individuals
Between us in our relationships and teams
Around us in the cultures we co-create and contribute to

CHAPTER EIGHT

Connecting the Practice to the Three Dimensions

My whole life, I have been known for my energy. Remember what my fourth-grade teacher said about me being the spice? I certainly do. Despite this, for many years what people experienced on the outside was not what I was experiencing on the inside. On the outside, I was a consummate pleaser, performer, and perfecter. On the inside, I was often experiencing significant strain, swirl, and stuck going even deeper into depression and anxiety.

This disconnect came at great cost to me being who I wanted to be in the world and the impact and influence I desired to have in it. Because while my energy literally vibrated the potential that was within me, I was deeply steeped in a problem mindset and its accompanying states of strain, swirl, and stuck. This made me someone who either backed away from opportunities that would make my potential shine or experienced them as a way to further beat myself up with my "not enough" words—not enough pleasing, not enough performing, not enough perfecting.

Through years of lifesaving and enriching professional support, an amazing husband who loved me so deeply it hurt at times because tough love was a real thing, profound learning, and practice, practice, practice, I have significantly shifted my operating system. Through shifting my thinking, feeling, and action again and again, I now spend much more time in a potential mindset rather than a problem one. Me being "the personality defect" or the "the problem" is no longer a world that my words create for me.

And I have done this by making the Connecting Potential Core Practice of "Intend, Notice, and Move" *the* core practice, not only in my work, but in my life by practicing it again and again, hardwiring it into my operating system.

Because I never take my mental health and vitality for granted, I am humbled and grateful to write these words as someone who is now integrated and connected in her core and whose outer worlds and inner actions are now congruent—through all the ups and downs. As a result, not only do others comment on my continuing energy, they also appreciate that I am real, and this realness resonates for greater connection, impact, and influence. The night before I wrote these words, a wonderful colleague said to me, "You come across as someone who has lived life fully and with that a great respect for it."

When I started writing this book, I knew that there were three key things I wanted to teach:

- a mindset that may be a *problem* or *potential* one

- an operating system with three core functions of *action, feeling,* and *thinking*

- a practice to connect it of *Intend, Notice,* and *Move*

I also knew that there were three dimensions where potential was always present—ready and waiting to be connected, within us, between us, and around us. Intuitively, I knew that all these pieces were connected, but I couldn't clearly articulate how. As I was writing my manuscript, it was through the conversations that I had working with my clients, the messages that I shared through keynote speaking engagements, and the insights from my powerful conversations with my coaches that these connections became clearer along with the words to share them with you now.

The revision and editing of this book required me to further synthesize decades of learning into teachings that were clear, compelling, and sticky for you, my reader. What became even clearer to me through this process is that despite the unique circumstances of each situation, challenge, or problem, the way to move through what is in the way and connect the potential there with greater energy, ease, and effectiveness in the process is the Connect Potential Practice of "Intend, Notice, and Move." And this practice has impact in all three dimensions of potential—within us, between us, and around us, because our operating systems (thinking, feeling, action) continue to operate in them.

WITHIN US—THE DIMENSION OF PERSONAL IMPACT

So far, we've focused on connecting potential in the first dimension "within us as individuals." Because it is you the individual here reading this book, and we each are our own most significant catalysts of connecting potential within, between, and around us when we make the choice to do so. I think this twist on the well-known Serenity Prayer captures the role we each hold:

Grant me the serenity to accept the ones I cannot change.

The courage to change the ones I can.

And the wisdom to know it's me.

Yes, "the wisdom to know it's me" is critical, remembering that as "control freaks" we want to control so much more, yet we don't. To quote one of my mentors, "You're it. No one else is coming." Okay, I am here with you, so while you need to do the work, you don't need to do it alone! I know that you are up to this opportunity and responsibility to dive deeper into connecting the potential within us.

The potential within us is with us all our lives. It shows up for each of us as uniquely as we each are—with a special combination of traits, experiences, learnings, and expressions of them in our worlds. I am happy to share stories of two amazing individuals who have connected and continue to connect the potential in the first dimension (within themselves) through the practice of Intend, Notice, and Move—and inspire me every day. Through their stories I highlight how they used the Connect Potential Practice (Intend, Notice, and Move) in ways that are as unique as they each are. It was so hard to choose just two, so you can find more amazing stories on the Community Hub.

THREE TIMES "NO!"...THREE EMMYS LATER

Jeff August (my younger brother) has not only won three Emmys for his work in creating amazing television through design, editorial, visual effects, and animation, he was won hundreds of awards and is known around the world as one of the best at what he does. As partner and creative director of Jump Studios, Jeff is a "unicorn" in his field because of his unique combination of creative and technical skills and ability to translate ideas and inspirations into creative, cohesive, and compelling media experiences. And it almost didn't happen! Before he even had a chance to connect his potential in his field, he was told "no" three times by the program that was the doorway into it—and that wasn't the only obstacle.

I joke that Jeff came out of the womb wanting to work in television because he was obsessed with it—he might have missed a year of university because of Much Music videos. He also always had the need to express himself, whether it was through entertaining others, often through the ridiculous stories he loved to tell, being a member of the band Jacuzzi Romance in the late '80s (yep, that was the actual name—the other one on the table was Floaties in the Pool), and then setting his sights on working in the television industry. While Jeff is not seen as someone who takes himself seriously—he has the best laugh in the world and you can hear it often—he has always taken his passion very seriously, key to him connecting his potential within himself.

Upon graduating from high school, he put his intention into action by applying for the Cinema, Television, Stage, and Radio (CTSR) program at SAIT in Calgary. This was a highly subscribed, highly competitive program that he was rejected from, not once, not twice, but three times, with each time being a devastating experience for him. Many others would have given up and decided to go another direction, but not Jeff. Instead, each time, he noticed and acknowledged his deep disappointment, and then made the moves to prepare himself for success. In Jeff's story, "move" was less about physical movement in the moment (I am still working on getting him to move his body more!), but rather about the moves he needed to make to prepare himself for success. These moves involved hours upon hours of volunteer work in the industry and forming the relationships he needed for success. He was determined, and it paid off. Jeff was not only admitted into the program, but he is also one of their most successful graduates, winning alumni of the year in 2004. In fact, his son, inspired by Jeff, graduated from the same program!

Speaking of graduation, Jeff skipped his to get his first job, a junior role at a local TV station with a salary that didn't cover his monthly expenses. He was in the industry that he loved and not having the impact that he desired. A record snowstorm changed all that. CBS sports was in Calgary doing a show and no one at the station wanted to work over the weekend. Jeff saw the potential and took on the work. As a result of being snowed in with CBS all weekend, Jeff became convinced that he needed to take his work to this level and not leave it local. CBS was convinced he was talent that they needed and within weeks he was in Lillehammer, Norway, creating the openings for the 1994 Olympics prime-time broadcasts. This was the Olympics of the Tonya Harding and Nancy Kerrigan drama and his opening for the women's figure skating final was the most watched two minutes of television at that time. There were only fourteen channels then, but I am sure you get that this was a big deal. A boy from Calgary won his first of three Emmys and his impact was worldwide!

And Jeff's journey to success is like most journeys are—always forward and never straight! In a highly competitive and always-changing industry, a VUCA one (volatile, uncertain, complex, and ambiguous), over the years he has had to keep his edge to remain successful, and he has by constantly being conscious in his intention, noticing his experience, and then making his next move. When I asked him what that looked like for him, he said:

My intention has always been to create amazing content that inspires people and *gives them goosebumps* like ABC's *Wide World of Sports* (you can Google it) did for me as a kid. I pay attention to (notice) who I surround myself with—people who have the same energy or benefit from mine. And I see myself as a chef who looks at the ingredients he is given and then creates the most special meal—one that you lose yourself in (move). I am driven to create positive energy and pay respect to what I fell in love with as a kid—music videos and sports TV (intend).

I hope that you feel the respect and appreciation I have for my brother, and his amazing journey "jumps" off the page much like his work at Jump Studios jumps off screens around the world. And Jeff, when you read this, remember to thank me when you pick up your first Academy Award!

WITH LOVE FROM JAMEY—I HAD TO NEARLY DIE IN ORDER TO LIVE

Jamey and I worked together at WestJet in the People and Culture Department. She was a powerful presenter and facilitator, known for her insight, energy, and ability to easefully build relationships with others to connect their potential in every interaction. She was also at a place in her career where she knew that she wanted to have greater influence and impact and was taking the steps to do so. On October 1, 2010, everything changed, as Jamey was the victim of a dangerous driver who sideswiped her at a busy intersection through an illegal left-hand turn. Jamey had to be removed from her car with the jaws of life and was lucky to be alive. Thankfully, she "only" suffered a severe concussion and soft-tissue injuries. They were devastating, however, keeping her from returning to full-time work for not weeks or months, but years. Her physical, mental, and emotional healing from this horrific event was arduous and unpredictable, but that is not her story.

Her story is how this awful accident and the repercussions from it to this day led her on a journey to fully discover who she is, what matters most to her, and the real difference she is here to make. Jamey can tell it much better than me, so let's hear from her:

What I had known to be a good life—a successful career and the material things that show you are successful—wasn't it. While they can contribute to it, they are not the bones. The bones are the relationships and the connections, who and what you love, and how you fill your days. *And* how you nourish your soul and your body (intend). Something greater was whispering to me—okay, at times, speaking loudly. So I disconnected from things that weren't really serving me anymore, and that included moving to a plant-based diet (move). Food has always been a big expression of my love, and I realized that when I ate in ways that didn't align with my values it wasn't nourishing me or others (notice).

In May of 2022, Jamey, myself, and three other close friends were on a girls' trip in New York. On our final day, during a walk on the Highline, Jamey shared with me that she had a friend who asked her to make plant-based meals for him and she wasn't sure what to do. Our conversation then went something like this:

- I asked her how this request aligned with what she wanted to do in the world. (Intend, Notice)

- She told me that while it did, it also made her a bit scared, and she was unsure how to do it. (Notice)

- I asked her what excited her about it, and she said because it aligned with her love for health, plant-based diets, and nourishing others. (Intend)

- I suggested that she take a deep breath, give it a go, and see what happened. (Breathe, Move)

Within weeks, she put her offering out into the world. With Love From Jamey creates and shares beautiful plant-based meals made with love for over a hundred nourished clients (and growing!). Her clients share that they can taste the love in her food, and when they open the fridge, they know she is supporting them. She also has several partnerships with whole foods providers, shares her wisdom and love of nourishment through her Instagram page, and she's not done connecting potential yet! If I have my way, some time soon, you will be reading and hearing more about her story along with amazing, nourishing recipes made with love in Jamey's book and the messages she shares with others. There, Jamey, I have put it out into the world for you! You can find her URL on the Community Hub and I encourage you to follow her on Instagram (withlovefromJamey). She inspires and nourishes me in every interaction, and I know that she will do that for you as well. Because for Jamey it is more than the business of preparing food. Here's how she puts it:

> "Living a good life. I always dreamed of having a home where people would pop in and I always have food. That is what I love about meal pick-up night. Somehow there are a minimum of three customers who have become friends sitting around the dining table sharing our passion for connection and living well. And I see this passion growing and having bigger impact."

I am grateful Jamey and I have a standing once-a-week prep date where we chop, cook, share our passions, connecting the potential that lives between us.

While these two stories were not free of challenges, problem mindsets, or strain, swirl, or stuck, the potential connectors in them embodied and continue to embody what it is to connect the potential within them by intending, noticing, and moving through it all. They inspire me and, I imagine, you as well!

YOUR CONNECTING POTENTIAL "WITHIN YOU" JOURNEY

On the Community Hub, you will find the Connect Potential Within Me Deep Dive Exercise that builds from the "Intend, Notice, and Move" core practice to go deeper in connecting the potential within yourself. For now, I leave you with three questions to percolate and journal on:

Intend: What is the "within me experience" that I want and the influence and impact that I desire to have? To be... so that I...

Notice: To what extent am I connecting this potential within me right now? (1–10) What words would I use to describe the experience within me?

Move: What is the next action I will take to move forward? (Always remember the power of just three breaths!)

Connecting potential within ourselves as individuals is a powerful launch point to connect potential in the other two dimensions, so let's move onto the next dimension—connecting the potential between us—the dimension of relational impact.

CONNECTING THE POTENTIAL BETWEEN US—THE DIMENSION OF RELATIONAL IMPACT

I completed my Master of Arts in Leadership degree in 2019. The program of study was through Royal Roads University (RRU), whose tag phrase is "life changing." My learning experience in this program lived up to that promise as it was the catalyst for me to leave my career of fourteen years with WestJet and start my performance practice of Connecting Potential.

During my studies we spent a lot of time learning about what we experience any time humans come together—relational systems and dynamics. These complex relationship systems (and the operating systems—thinking, feeling, acting—in them) constantly emerge and change in unpredictable ways making them interesting, challenging, frustrating, and messy much of the time. While I am so appreciative of my learning through this degree, I graduated with many interesting insights and no idea how to leverage them in a meaningful way. That was until I discovered the method that I am now certified in as a systems coach—Organization and Relationship Systems Coaching (ORSC). A core tenet of ORSC is that relationship systems are naturally intelligent, creative, and generative—core beliefs that align with and point to the potential that lives between us in our relationships and teams.

Because in any relationship system, be it a work or personal one, with one other person or with several, there exists something between us—a dynamic that ORSC refers to as the "third entity." In any relationship system, there are the parts, the people who make it up, and the whole, the relationship itself or third entity.

If I just lost you on that last point, imagine this for a moment. You are in a busy restaurant with every table full. As you look around the restaurant to see what is happening (one of my favorite pastimes—I call it "curious"—my husband calls it "nosy"), you notice different dynamics happening at different tables. For example, at one table you see a young couple who are clearly enjoying time with each other, and the word that comes to mind is "intimate." At another you see a family with several small children and lots of activity, and the word you use to describe that table is "harried." And finally, at another, you see deep conversation happening with a small group that you characterize as "intense." What you have just experienced in this visualization is the dynamic that lives between us or the third entity, a dynamic that is its own thing and a source of potential. Another way to describe how this dynamic shows up is when we watch a sporting event and can distinctly see and feel which team has chemistry, which one does not, and when momentum shifts from one to the other in a game or a match.

Most of the relationships, one-on-one or in teams, that I am asked to coach are already performing, sometimes despite the dynamic between them causing the states of strain, swirl, or stuck. I am asked to help solve a problem in the dynamic between the people in them—the disconnect in their operating system—thinking, feeling, and actioning between them. Sometimes—no, often—that problem is identified as one or more of the members of it. I have found time and time again in these situations that the problem is not just in the individuals, but rather in the dynamic, misalignment, and missed opportunities to connect the potential between them. In these situations, I am always amazed, but never surprised, that once that dynamic is revealed and the potential uncovered, how quickly the relationship or team can move forward with greater energy, ease, and effectiveness.

There are several great books written about building strong relationships and teams, including *Fierce Conversations* by Susan Scott. Her notion of the power of conversations informed how I have framed this book, as a series of conversations, with most of the conversations so far being ones between you and me and ones that I am asking you to have with yourself.

Susan Scott goes as far to say that conversations are so important to relationships that they *are* the relationship. Our relationships go as our conversations go: If our conversations are open, our relationships are open. If our conversations are guarded, our relationships are guarded. If our conversations are strained, swirling, or stuck, our relationships are strained, swirling, or stuck. This results in problem mindsets not only for the individuals in the relationship, but the relationship itself. On the other hand, when potential is connected between us in our relationships and teams, our conversations and our relationships are ones of energy, ease, and effectiveness.

Because the conversations we have between us are such a powerful opportunity to connect the potential that is there, the stories I share next focus on specific conversations I coached and facilitated with two teams that (no surprise) contain the core practice elements of "Intend, Notice, and Move."

A TEAM THAT BREATHES TOGETHER, GETS REAL TOGETHER

I recently facilitated a session with sixty global leaders, a combination of directors, VPs, and executives. It was a challenging time in their sector, and the team needed to engage in critical conversations to address problems facing the organization. As the facilitator, I knew this would be particularly tricky because of the large size of the group. There are not many of us who love speaking up in a group of sixty, even those in leadership roles, so I designed the session to include "safer" modes of contribution including small group conversations with my favorite facilitation tools—post-it notes and flipchart paper. I also needed to fulfill a specific request from the executive team to get more voices participating in the large group conversations, so I designed the session using "Intend, Notice, and Move."

I worked with the executive team prior to the session to be clear not only on their desired outcomes for the meeting, but how they intended to show up as the most senior leaders of the organization. Their intentions centered around being "clear, open, listening, and receptive," and they shared these intentions with the broader team at the start of the session. I then facilitated a conversation where we surfaced the intentions of the team, which were largely aligned with those of the executive team, along with an intention to actively contribute their thinking and perspectives to the larger conversation. We were off to a good start, but I knew that these intentions would be "simple and not easy": simple to say, but not easy to do, once conversations got uncomfortable.

And they became uncomfortable very quickly as there were divergent, conflicting perspectives in the room, an uncomfortable yet necessary part of the group problem-solving process—sometimes called the "groan zone." The team became misaligned in intention and action. Instead of contributions there were "crickets." Instead of eye contact with each other, eyes went down to admire the pattern of the carpet in the room. Instead of "leaning in" to contribute to the conversation, leaders were awkwardly shifting in their seats. It was clear the team was stuck.

When I introduced the power of noticing to you, I shared the reality that whether we notice our experience or not, it is already happening. Only when we notice our experience are we at choice on what to do next. I shared this insight with the leadership team and I could see it resonated, also normalizing what was happening. I then shared what I noticed when things got "crunchy"—crickets, carpet, and contribution (or lack thereof)—and asked them how close my observations were to what they noticed. Their nods to each *c* as I shared it let me know right away that what I noticed was what was happening. I then reminded the team of the intentions they shared for their participation at the beginning of the session and the "wonderful opportunity" (we coaches and facilitators can be really annoying when things get tough) that the team had because of the creative tension that existed between what the team intended and what they noticed was happening here and now.

At that point, I had several choices about where to go next. I could have unpacked with the team what was making them hold back, asked them where they wanted to go next, or just carried on. I did none of those things; instead I took the team through a group breathwork exercise to help them get unstuck. *What?! You did breathwork with a team of sixty senior leaders at a business meeting?* I did, and here's why—the body always wins.

For a moment, let's go back to our conversation about our Connect Potential Operating System. Remember our "hand" model of the brain where the three core functions and parts are? Our action brain stem, feeling limbic system, and thinking cortex? You have likely experienced a time where despite your best intention going into a situation, something or, more likely, someone set you off and you went from a place of connection to disconnection and from potential to problem. Why this happens and happens so quickly is because this system is designed to act, feel, and then think, in that order. We are wired to be safe first, and actions keep us safe. We feel second because the amygdala hot button lets us know if safety actions are required. And we think last, at least conscious thoughts, because in a threatening situation there is no time to think it through. When we perceive a threat, most often unconsciously, our fight-or-flight reaction is automatically activated in the sympathetic nervous system, with all its physical manifestations that get in the way of connecting our thoughts, feelings, and actions in an intentional way—"the body always wins." The fastest and most effective way to interrupt this reaction is with the simply powerful tool we have with us in every moment, our breath practice.

Now back to the team and doing breathwork with sixty senior leaders. Even though the team set clear, shared intentions for how they wanted to engage with each other, the moment it got difficult in the large room those intentions got stuck. The operating system of the team disconnected, and I decided in that moment the right next move was a physical one to reset it. Together we did the three-breath practice, while I explained the science behind it to give it much-needed validity and credibility. And it worked.

While there were nervous glances and uncomfortable laughter as we began, by the time we finished three rounds of three breaths like you did in the Connect Potential Core Practice, the room dramatically shifted. It went from feeling constricted and stuck to open and responsive. The intentions set by the team at the beginning of the session came alive again. We took a short break to give everyone time to integrate the shift and shake off whatever else remained and came back to the conversation. My challenge as a facilitator went from working hard to draw out contributions to moving quickly to keep up with them and keep the conversation moving in a productive way. Was everything that leaders said easy to say and easy to hear? No, the conversations got heated at times, yet the team stayed committed to contributing to them and open to listening what was being said.

The team marveled at the end of the day, not only about how much they accomplished, but also commented that it was the first time they had been that open and real with each other in the large group context, and while challenging it was energizing. Having said that, as we started the second day of the session, one of the executive leaders said, "Okay, Pam, let's just get into it today. We don't have time to breathe." To which I responded, "And how's that working out?" After the laughter in the room subsided, we did three quick breaths together and got to work.

YOU'RE ON MUTE

The second story I want to share with you about connecting potential between us happened when I was brought in to help an IT department co-create their future vision, along with the strategies to achieve it. They were a talented team of individuals with diverse backgrounds and skillsets who shared a common purpose (intend) of helping the business and their clients be more successful with IT as a strategic and seamless tool. When I asked them how close they were to living it now, the average response was a four out of ten because they were frustrated that the business saw them as "order takers" rather than partners and collaborators, and this was making them feel strained and stuck— unable to fully execute on their strategy (notice).

Through our conversations, I noticed a pattern in their team dynamic where it took a long time for anyone to speak up, requiring repeated prompting by me. This particularly became evident in one conversation where I needed to say "you're on mute" four times as a team member fumbled to unmute themselves. When we finally heard from this team member, what they said was a key to the challenge the IT team was experiencing with the business—because it was what they were experiencing between themselves in their team dynamic. The team member said, "I'm so sorry it took me so long. I don't have the muscle memory to unmute myself in team meetings, because I'm not usually asked to contribute to them." It was the "mic drop" moment in the session, because how could the team be effective partners and collaborators outside of their team if they didn't do it inside between themselves? This was the potential that wanted and needed to be connected.

I let some silence do the heavy lifting and, after a long pause, asked the team what was happening in the dynamic after their colleague's comment. The blinding flash of the obvious for the group was that they saw that they couldn't be partners and collaborators with the business if they couldn't be that between themselves. I then asked them where else the lack of space and/or reluctance to contribute showed up in their team dynamic (further noticing) and what they wanted to happen between them instead (intend). They were able to identify the problem pattern that they were in—using team conversations as a space to report and receive information rather than collaborate and solve problems with each other. It showed up several places, and they wanted and needed this to change, particularly because it mattered that they be seen as partners and collaborators with the business. I invited the team to take a breath and exhale before asking them what they wanted to do with that insight. They did and then created an agreement to invite and make space for every voice along with a commitment to speak up when it was their voice that needed to be heard (move). In my next conversation with them, I had no issues getting team members to participate and contribute—in fact there was a queue of digital hands waiting for their turn. While not part of the official vision and strategy planning support they asked me for, the potential that was connected between them in that moment (we make space for contribution and step up to offer it) was a connection that carried forward in their con-versations, team dynamic, and ultimately effectiveness as a partner and collaborator with the business.

YOUR CONNECTING POTENTIAL "BETWEEN YOU" JOURNEY

On the Community Hub, you will find a Relationships Potential Pulse where you can reflect on a relationship or team in your work or life that matters to you. You can also check on the pulse of the potential between you, along with suggested actions to connect it further. For now, here are three questions to reflect on:

Intend: What is the "between us experience" that I want and the influence and impact that I desire us to have? To be... so that I...

Notice: To what extent we are connecting this potential between us right now? (1–10) What words would I use to describe the experience between us?

Move: What is the next action we might take to move forward? (Remember that teams can breathe together!)

Or better yet, have this conversation with the other person or team members, replacing the word *I* with *we.* Oh, and one more thing about the potential that lives between us. It would all be easier if no people were involved—easier, perhaps, but certainly less energizing! This statement is even truer as we layer in the complexity that comes with more individuals, more relationships, and more teams in organizations and the culture that is constantly co-created around them—a culture that can both connect and disconnect potential.

CONNECTING THE POTENTIAL AROUND US—THE DIMENSION OF ORGANIZATIONAL IMPACT

"We have lost our culture." This was a statement that I heard many times in my fourteen years at WestJet and continue to hear from many of the cultures that I work with now. And while culture is a dynamic that is constantly changing and evolving, sometimes the way we want and sometimes not, I find the statement "we lost (or are losing) our culture" problematic because it implies that culture is something we have, something that can be given or taken away by someone else. After hearing this statement countless times, I started replying by asking, "Where did it go? Is it under the table? In your backpack? Over there in the corner?" Because culture is not a "thing" that can be lost or found, it is the way and the why we do everything.

Culture is not what happens at team events or meetings or social hours (or what I sometimes refer to as the "three Ps of culture"—ping pong, potlucks, or parties) although they can be activators of it. It is the dynamic that is constantly co-created in the time and space between these activations—every day, in every action and every interaction, by everyone. I had a conversation with a leader recently at one of my keynote messages around developing culture by design rather than default who said, "We don't have a culture." To which I responded, "Oh, but you do—you just aren't aware of it. And if you don't notice what is already happening, you can't intentionally be at choice about what to do about it." (Notice "Intend, Notice, and Move" in my response?) And while leaders play a critical role in shaping organizational culture, it is not "owned" by any one person. It is owned by each member of its co-creation, whether they pay attention to it or not.

Culture at its core is a system of learning. Because in every culture we are part of there is a constant learning of what the shared beliefs, values, behaviors, and practices (thinking, feeling, action) are with a group of people. Not by values on glossy posters, screensavers, or plaques on the wall, but by the way things *really* get done *every* day, in *every* action, and *every* interaction. I repeated this on purpose to stress the "every-ness" of culture. In my performance practice, I work with organizational cultures, helping these relationship systems connect the potential that lives around them. And this process is complex— as the operating systems of the individuals (within them dimension) and teams (between them dimension) are also operating at the same time. Sometimes in alignment—sometimes not. The challenge I see most often is the misalignment between intention and action that goes unnoticed. This challenge reminds me of another one of my favorite quotes, "While I judged myself by my intentions, the world was judging me by my actions." (Bill W.)

Saying that culture is "the way we do things" is an oversimplification in part because it doesn't capture the real drivers of culture as discussed by Edgar Schein, thought leader in organizational culture: our underlying beliefs and assumptions. The reasons why we—often unconsciously—think things happen the way they do. Working with organizational cultures is particularly tricky because the things that have the greatest impact on them are largely unconscious, invisible, and implicit, leading to all kinds of misalignments and misinterpretations. As I shared earlier in the book, when speaking about culture, I often use the metaphor of water, because much like a fish doesn't know that they are in water (I recognize that this is an assumption on my part), we often don't notice the potential that lives around us in the culture that we are in because it is the "water" we are in.

To connect it, we need to make the unconscious conscious, invisible visible, and the implicit explicit. And this task often feels daunting because it is challenging enough to deal with what we do know, see, and hear. So we stick to the things that we can immediately experience (and sometimes check off a list)—things like team building events, social hours, or the three Ps (ping pong, potlucks, and parties). And then we are surprised when we don't achieve what we know we can based on the potential that we know is there around us. A core part of my role when I work with cultures as a systems coach and consultant is to help them make the shifts from unconsciousness to consciousness, invisible to visible, and implicit to explicit.

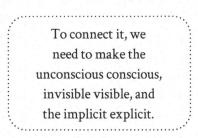

To connect it, we need to make the unconscious conscious, invisible visible, and the implicit explicit.

I have a card on my desk, a quote by Oscar Wilde that says, "Be yourself because everyone else is taken." This statement is not only true for individuals, but for organizational cultures as well. The goal is not to be someone else but rather to move forward the best of who you are as a culture, while developing into the best of who you want and need to be—this is the essence of what it means to connect potential around us in cultures. And that is what the organizations in the next two stories have done and continue to do, intending, noticing, and moving along the way.

THE BEST WAY TO PREDICT THE FUTURE IS TO *CO-CREATE* IT

The best way to predict the future is to *co-create* it. This is what Rümi (pronounced "roomie") did as they built their culture and launched a new brand and service offering into the market during the pandemic. A brand within the ATCO Energy global organization, Rümi's purpose is both simple and significant: "to make people happy by making it easier for everyone to love the places they live or work." The senior team at Rümi saw the critical connection between brand and culture that I frame like this. Brand is the *external* promise that a company makes to the world, and culture is how they come together *internally* to deliver on that promise. I was brought in as a culture specialist with the marketing-engagement firm Cult Ideas to partner with the organization to develop and activate their core culture framework and roadmap in late 2019. It was a good thing that nothing was going on in the world as we dove deep into this important and ambitious task in early 2020!

From the start of the work to today, intentional co-creation is the way things get done at Rümi. We engaged the voices and perspectives of all "Rümineers" in all aspects of the framework design and roadmap activation. This included the name and identity they gave themselves to represent their spirit of "forging new paths." When "two weeks" of COVID lockdown stretched into two months and then two years, the leadership team at Rümi never wavered from their commitment to co-creating *with* their people rather than doing *to* them. They took the time—time and time again—to pause, notice, and move where their people and the culture wanted and needed to go. And it paid off.

Fast forward to 2024, Rümi's business is thriving with customer conversion rates high and net promoter scores (customers' likelihood to recommend) "through the roof." What else would you expect from a "call center" that is named the Customer Care Happiness Centre? When the CFO from ATCO, the parent company, spent a day with the team there, he reported back that it was "truly the happiest place on earth." While Rümi has already shifted and adapted their business strategy in response to customer needs and what the market is asking for, the culture core has remained constant because constant at Rümi means staying grounded in purpose and adapting and moving forward together.

Nicole Murray, Rümi's People and Culture Champion (how cool is that title?), told me the story that her happiest days at work are four Fridays a year—not for the reason you may think. While many organizations have recognition programs, at Rümi, appreciation is something that is done intentionally every day. Their culture of appreciation culminates each quarter with their peer recognition ÜShine Awards. Each and every quarter, approximately 70 out of Rümi's 170-member team nominate a peer for an award. While not everyone can win the quarterly award drawn from the nominees, on that Friday, Nicole sends each nominee their submission from their fellow Rümineer with a personal note from herself. TGIF! On the note of personal notes, Rümi's president sends postcards of appreciation to team members' homes so that their families can also see them appreciated by "the big boss."

Finally, imagine a workplace where team members invite colleagues from other departments to come listen to live calls with customers? At Rümi, their ÜListen initiative does this so that all Rümineers have an opportunity to hear right from the customer and experience the connection created as Rümi's culture flows through the phone lines. And Happiness Centre agents love hosting. Intentional co-creation and noticing and moving together fuels an energy and culture that gets results, and gets recognized as one of Canada's Most Admired Corporate Cultures. Bravo to Rümi and all Rümineers who make it happen.

WE JUST MOVED!

"People Flourish Here" is more than a mantra or a slogan. It is the lived cultural experience of Lavender, another amazing organization I am fortunate to work with. It is also the experience they come together to create for their clients through mental health medication management and therapy support delivered by a team of psychiatric nurse practitioners. And they do all of this through services that are delivered 100 percent virtually with a fully remote operations team in Canada, nurse practitioners in the US, and concierge team in the Philippines. When asked how Lavender grew from just three client visits in their first month of operation in May 2020 to thousands per month four years later, Lavender's co-founders Pritma Dhillon-Chattha and Brighid Gannon's answer was simple: "We just moved!"

Pritma and Brighid met while completing their Doctor of Nursing Practice in Leadership and Healthcare Management degrees at Yale University. During March 2020, both of their brick-and-mortar businesses shut down. Seeing and hearing a need for access to mental health services (notice) they saw an opportunity to do something different and important in the mental health space (intend) and they *just moved*. In the US psychiatric nurse practitioners fill an important gap in the care of mental health, and the pandemic lockdowns created the potential to fulfill this need virtually. They brought together their education and experience along with a small team of psychiatric nurse practitioners who were out of work due to care facility lockdowns. Necessity required that they move fast. And they did, launching Lavender in New York state after just forty-five days! While their focus was on moving, iterating, and pivoting quickly as a start-up business, through it all Lavender's co-founders aligned on what mattered most—creating therapeutic journeys that are kind, convenient, and transparent so that people can flourish—now Lavender's mission. With this clear intention, every day they moved and moved again, inviting others who shared this passion into the journey. They concerned themselves more with doing something rather than doing it perfectly, creating space for others to do the same. In doing so, they led the co-creation of a culture where people do flourish inside and outside of the organization.

I started working with Lavender during the spring of 2022, designing and facilitating their team retreat in New York. For many on the team, it was the first time that they ever came together face-to-face. If I didn't know that going in, I would have never known that this was a remote team because of their strong connection with each other and alignment on what matters most—people flourishing. I quickly saw that part of Lavender's DNA was the intention of "generous assumption" that continues to move through their culture, the belief that each member intends to contribute their best even when their actions fall short. And according to the co-founders, "the practice of making generous assumptions just makes your own life easier. If you start an interaction with someone from that belief, the interaction is more effortless." Sounds a lot like a potential mindset and connected operating systems (act, feel, think) experiencing ease, doesn't it? It is also an essential ingredient to build the deep trust needed for a successful virtual team. And it creates the conditions around its people to connect their potential in delivering above-and-beyond services in the mental health space, putting hospitality back into healthcare in a real and sincere way.

While Lavender's culture is what the co-founders are most proud of—with an overall engagement and *say, stay, strive* score of 92 percent—it is also what they are most concerned about (notice) as they continue to grow beyond the six states they now provide care in. Their continued focus is on building the connective tissue between and around them with team cohesion as one of their strategic pillars, and I am grateful to support them in this important work.

YOUR CONNECTING POTENTIAL "AROUND YOU" JOURNEY

Once again on the Community Hub you will find the Culture Roadmap Framework that I use when I work with organizations so you can see the rigid minimal structure ("RMS") that I use to meet culture systems where they are and help them connect the potential around them as they develop into who they need to be. I also share some self-serve culture tools that you can use within your organization. For now, here are three more questions. Think of a culture system that you are part of and reflect on:

Intend: What is the "around us experience" that I want and the influence and impact that I desire us to have as a culture? To be...so that we...

Notice: To what extent we are connecting this potential around us right now? (1–10) What words would members use to describe the culture experience around us?

Move: What is the next action we might take to move forward? (Cultures can also take a breath in a metaphoric sense.)

CONNECTING POTENTIAL IN THREE DIMENSIONS

I hope that you now believe that it is possible to connect potential in each of the three dimensions and are energized to do so. While the work is often challenging because it would be easy if no people were involved (easier and much less fulfilling), it can be more energetic, easeful, and effective. How? By *intending, noticing, and moving* to connect the potential that is already there in each dimension just waiting to be connected.

I invite you to pause and reflect on the following question before we move on to our final two chapters together. Feel free to grab your journal and write down your reflections.

> When I connected potential in one dimension, how did it contribute to potential being connected in the other two dimensions?

When I connected potential in one dimension, how did it contribute to potential being connected in the other two dimensions?

I ask this now, because by connecting potential in any one dimension, you create the opportunity (or potential) to connect it in all three. Said another way: when you influence anything, you influence everything. This is the promise of connecting potential. Let's explore why this is true, and how to make it happen.

POTENTIAL

ONE Mindset Shift

**From *Problem* to *Potential*,
grounding in what matters**

ONE Operating System

ACT, FEEL, THINK

Disconnected Operating System =
Strain, Swirl, Stuck

- **Strain:** I can move, but it is hard and it hurts.
- **Swirl:** I can't stop but I am getting nowhere.
- **Stuck:** I can't move.

Connected Operating System =
Energy, Ease, Effectiveness

- **Energy:** I have energy to move; each move energizes me!
- **Ease:** I am relaxed and full of ease.
- **Effectiveness:** My actions lead to the outcomes I desire.

ONE Core Practice

INTEND, NOTICE, MOVE

Intend draws us forward.

Notice grounds us to take the first step.

The **creative tension** between the two gives us energy to move,

Move gets us from where we are to where we want to go.

THREE Dimensions of Exponential Impact

INTEND, NOTICE, MOVE

Within us as individuals

Between us in our relationships and teams

Around us in the cultures we co-create and contribute to

CHAPTER NINE

Influence Anything, Influence Everything

A t fourteen, our youngest son, Jarrett, an air cadet with dreams of one day going to space, applied to receive an aerospace scholarship for a coveted summer program. As part of his preparation, I got him a ten-minute telephone interview with Chris Hadfield. If you don't know who Chris is, he is a former astronaut and the first Canadian to hold command of the international space station. So to get time for my son to speak with him was a great "mom moment!" Our son prepared his questions for Chris and asked if it was okay for him to record the conversation, Chris graciously said yes, and the ten-minute timer started. Ten minutes turned into over an hour as Chris and our son engaged in an in-depth and inspiring conversation about Chris's career and our son's aspirations. Because our son was so well prepared and obviously committed to connecting his potential, Chris let him know they could talk as long as he had questions. Another proud mom moment!

It is Chris's answer to the question, "What was the hardest part of becoming an astronaut?" that best illustrates the power of connecting potential, not only in one dimension but all three. I paraphrase his answer as this: "The hardest part is that I set an impossible dream. And when you have an impossible dream, it changes who you are every day as you work to fulfill it." Or, in my language, connect that potential! You see, when Chris was nine, he decided that he wanted to walk on the moon. At that time, no one had. And while he never walked on the moon, in working to achieve this "impossible dream" he did fulfill his dreams of space travel and so much more. He continues to use his "beyond our world" insight and inspiration to inspire and influence generations. Added to the list of his accomplishments? Changing the life of our son with one conversation.

When the call was over, I looked at Jarrett and said, "Honey, I want you to remember this moment—how this call made you think, how it made you feel, and your physical experience right now—because this call has changed your life." And it did. Jarrett didn't get the scholarship for the aerospace program, and while he was disappointed, it didn't crush him the way other so-called failures did because he remembered that while Chris "didn't make it to the moon, he did change the world"—my son's words, not mine.

Jarrett went on the next year to be selected as one of fifty youth from around the world to attend an international space program in Houston, Texas, became a member of the Canadian Armed Forces at age eighteen as an Air Force pilot, successfully completed his first phase of military flight training, earned a mechanical engineering degree, and as I write these words, is embarking on further military flight training as part of a NATO international pilot cohort. He is also now the role model for other young cadets giving back to the program that launched him. So the influence and impact of that conversation years ago continues to connect the potential within him as an individual, between him and his fellow military members, and around him in the military culture and broader worlds that he strives to impact for the better.

I share this story because one conversation changed the trajectory of the life of someone who matters a great deal to me. As you have already seen, I am a strong believer in Susan Scott's work around the power of conversations. I often share the following quote because it perfectly captures the power of just one conversation to connect potential for exponential impact and influence. It also so clearly amplifies the fact that when we influence anything, we influence everything.

"Our work, our relationships, and our lives succeed or fail one conversation at a time. While no single conversation is guaranteed to transform a company, a relationship, or a life, any single conversation can. Speak and listen as if this is the most important conversation you will ever have with this person. It could be. Participate as if it matters. It does."

One more Susan Scott wisdom that has really stuck with me and I am reminded of with my son's story is this notion of "gradually then suddenly." Someone doesn't *suddenly* win a gold medal. Overnight successes don't actually happen overnight, because in these situations it is a whole bunch of *gradually* that leads to a "suddenly" experience. In the case of the gold medal athlete, think of every workout, every repetition, every practice—all the hours, days, weeks, months it takes for them to reach competition, much less the podium. And in the case of the young learner (me) who built a successful career and life fulfilling her purpose, it didn't happen overnight. Rather, it happened one intention, one noticing, one movement at a time, time and time again. And it often didn't feel like it was happening at all! Even though it was.

This is another thing about gradually then suddenly. The very nature of gradually feels like you are not getting there, like you're going nowhere. This creates discomfort and tension, tension that can be a creative source of energy as it keeps us moving forward to what we intend, what we want, what we dream of. Our tendency can be to let our "lack of progress" turn into a problem that then can lead us into the three Ss. Instead, once again my encouragement to you is to see that the discomfort you may feel is a signal—the tension between where you are and where you want to be. The potential there that wants to be connected.

FOR MY MOTHER

This story is top of my mind and my heart as I share with you the exponential power of connecting potential in all three dimensions. My completion of the first draft of this manuscript had a firm deadline of

October 23, 2022. Not because anyone imposed it on me, but because it was a significant day. You see, October 23rd is my mom's birthday and my mom passed away after a short battle with cancer in early 2017. On this day, she would have been eighty-two. My mom and I had a very close relationship, and as our closest relationships often are, it was messy—at times really messy. There are no words to describe the pain, fear, and despair that followed her diagnosis of stage four cancer in the fall of 2016.

It was particularly a shock because she was so youthful and vibrant, and the story we all had in our heads is that she would be the ninety-five-year-old grandma—for sure. During the five months before she passed, there was not one doctor's visit that gave us good news, and after a particularly difficult one where her doctor told her to really savor Christmas with her family as it might be her last, it became too much. Right after the appointment, as we were at the supermarket pharmacy getting her pain meds, we took each other's hand walking down the cereal aisle (so strange the things we remember), and started to weep. Once we got into my car, I was overcome with sobbing, and my mom reached out to comfort me, saying, "I am okay, you know." I said, "I know—it's just that this really sucks." (I may have added in a rhyming word before *sucks* that starts with an *f*). And she said the following words that changed this terrible, horrific problem into the potential that shaped us and our relationship in a new way until her death and beyond:

"The situation sucks. But we don't suck in the situation."

And we didn't. Instead, we were there for each other, we loved each other, and when she left there was nothing missing between us. This experience not only changed our relationship, it changed me as a mom, a wife, a sister, a leader, a facilitator. In fact, when I shared this story on LinkedIn, Brené Brown said she was going to use it (just thought I might throw that in there). My mom's impact from connecting her potential through terminal cancer is wider than either of us could have ever imagined. She would love that Brené said she was going to share my words.

I share this story to remind you that potential is already there no matter the circumstance. It's within you, between you, and around you. When things get in the way, they *are* the way. When situations suck, you don't. This is true for me, it was true for my mom, and it is true for you too.

That instructor and her destructive words all those years ago were the way for me to see what I was really here to do in this world—connect potential. My challenges with depression and anxiety were the way for me to deepen my own learning and healing so that I could show others it was possible for them as well. Struggling to leave an organization and career that I loved was the way for me to get crystal clear on the work I needed to do to take my impact and influence to the world in a broader and deeper way. Going through the cancer battle with my mom connected within me that deep sorrow and deep joy do have space for each other.

Writing through each of the obstacles of creating this book and putting myself out to the world as an author is just another way for me to show you that what's in the way became the way for me to connect

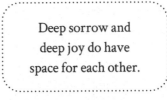

Deep sorrow and deep joy do have space for each other.

potential within myself. While through the process, I experienced it all: strain (*how can I ever keep going when there is so much going on?*), swirl (*too many ideas, insights, and experiences that can't possibly weave together!*), and stuck (*who do I think I am saying that I am an author—imposter syndrome!*). Yet here we are experiencing this book together.

And in doing so, we connected the potential that lives between us in our relationship as author and reader or one that I hope qualifies as friendship—either a new one if this is the first time we have met, or if we were already connected before you picked up this book, a deeper and richer one. I am confident that you will do same within you, between you, and around you. It's just how it works. That's the exponential power of connecting potential. All you need to do is Intend, Notice, and Move—again and again.

So let's go back to that learner at the beginning this book, the girl who was and is me. That horrible moment—those awful words, "You have a personality defect that will prevent you from ever being successful in life," could have resulted in a different story, one that would not have ended up in a book about connecting potential. But that experience was the moment that my operating system unconsciously at first made a powerful decision and set a powerful intention—"I will never make anyone feel the way that you made me feel. Anyone who ever connects with me will know that they have potential and that they can connect it."

I would love to say the rest of the story is, "She lived happily ever after from that moment forward"—no, wait a minute, I don't! Because if that were the case I would not have had the rich (often difficult) experiences and learning that came from them that brought me here today and connected with you through this book. And as I have often done throughout the experience of this book, I will invite you to pause and take a breath because while the journey of connecting potential with exponential impact (within, between, around) is an energetic one, there is no rush. You are exactly where you need to be right now. There is no hurry, because how it happens is gradually, then suddenly. And when we know that what we are doing matters and we matter as we do it, we stay grounded for the journey.

POTENTIAL

ONE Mindset Shift

**From *Problem* to *Potential*,
grounding in what matters**

ONE Operating System

ACT, FEEL, THINK

Disconnected Operating System =
Strain, Swirl, Stuck

Connected Operating System =
Energy, Ease, Effectiveness

- **Strain:** I can move, but it is hard and it hurts.
- **Swirl:** I can't stop but I am getting nowhere.
- **Stuck:** I can't move.

- **Energy:** I have energy to move; each move energizes me!
- **Ease:** I am relaxed and full of ease.
- **Effectiveness:** My actions lead to the outcomes I desire.

ONE Core Practice

INTEND, NOTICE, MOVE

Intend draws us forward.

Notice grounds us to take the first step.

The **creative tension** between the two gives us energy to move,

Move gets us from where we are to where we want to go.

THREE Dimensions of Exponential Impact

INTEND, NOTICE, MOVE

Within us as individuals

Between us in our relationships and teams

Around us in the cultures we co-create and contribute to

INFLUENCE ANYTHING, YOU INFLUENCE EVERYTHING

CHAPTER TEN

Mattering Matters

At the beginning of this book, I asked you to find an object that represents something that matters to you and reflect on what it represents. I asked you to do this at the beginning of our journey through the book together, because while potential energizes us, matter grounds us. And both are important. As a reminder, my synthesized definition of matter is below:

Matter *n.*

some "thing" of **substance** *and/or* **significance**

The words *substance* and *significance* are not only important because they ground us; I believe that they are conditions that matter for all of us in our journey of connecting potential. I wrote the following two statements on a post-it note and put it on my computer in 2020. The note is still there because the truth in these statements is still there:

"We all need to do something that matters" (substance)

"We all need to know that we matter as we do it" (significance)

When we can say "yes, I am doing something that matters" and "yes, I matter as I am doing it," that is when the magic that results from us connecting potential is most powerfully activated with energy, ease, and effectiveness. When we know that we matter, we become the catalyst and the creator that connects our potential, grounding it and making it even more real within us, between us, and around us. In every story that I shared throughout the book, "mattering" was there. Every situation had substance and significance that grounded potential so it could more powerfully be connected.

Now, I leave you with what is perhaps the most important action that you can take! Even if you forget everything else that you learned through this book (although I know that you won't because you have practiced along the way and practice makes—you got it—permanent!), you can take this with you. And here it is:

Create "moments of mattering" in your life. Let someone who matters to you know that they matter by sharing with them:

- What they are *doing* matters (substance)

- And *they* matter while they are doing it. (significance)

Every day, tell someone why you appreciate them and thank them for their impact—for their mattering.

THE NO-EGG IMPACT

I'll share one final story to show both the power of small actions and simple appreciation to make moments of mattering a real activator to connect potential.

A year ago, I was at a Denny's restaurant having breakfast with my family on a Saturday morning—which always presents a bit of a problem because I hate eggs, and *hate* is not an exaggeration. When I was a toddler, my mom was told that eggs were critical for my growth and development, so she forced me to eat them, not scrambled or in an omelette but in the jarred baby-food form. Gross! As a result, while I can eat eggs as an ingredient, I can't tolerate them as a dish and have never eaten them on their own since I was two years old. Back to the here and now and breakfast at Denny's.

While I hate eggs, the dishes on the menu that appeal to me are the ones with eggs as a centerpiece ingredient. So the conversation usually goes like this: "Could I have the breakfast scramble without the eggs?"

To which I am almost always met with a blank stare, sometimes a glare, and something like, "I am not sure...we will see what we can do." It's clear that my request is usually a problem. Not this time at Denny's! Our amazing server heard my question and said, "Absolutely!" She then let me know I mattered by saying, "Because you aren't having eggs, can I offer you another breakfast protein or perhaps a yogurt and fruit?" *What?!* Not only was I not being problematic, but she also showed me that I mattered by graciously making an offer that I had never received before (and I mean never!). I could not let this go by without creating another moment of mattering beyond the good tip.

When she brought me my breakfast, I said, "Thank you so much for offering me those choices. Thank you for making my breakfast experience such a great one. I really appreciate it." Both the smile on her face and her surprise in being appreciated by me, reinforced that the smallest moments can be the most important "moments of mattering" because not only do they have impact, we don't do them enough! I followed up by letting the restaurant manager know the difference that she made for me on my way out.

In a follow-up to this story, I recently facilitated a session on putting values into action with the Denny's leadership team. Denny's and the other amazing brands of Northland Properties are one of my clients. During the workshop I shared the "no egg" story with the leadership team as an example of small actions that have big impact. After the session, one of the leaders introduced himself as the manager I provided the appreciation to! He then shared that one year later, his server still recounts the story about the "no eggs" as an opportunity to create great experiences for their guests.

Mattering matters for much longer than the moment of mattering takes. (It's a mouthful—you might want to read that again.) Please take time today (and every day) to create a moment of mattering with someone who matters to you. It can be the old-fashioned way in person, or just pick up your phone and send a quick note. I know you have it close by, so use it for a good purpose.

NOT THE END

And finally, as we bookmark this part of our journey together, I hope that you know how much you matter to me. Thank you for trusting me on this journey and for committing to connecting the potential within you, between you, and around you. If you are here now, I know that you are committed and it's already happening.

I feel like we have connected through the words of this book and that through our conversations, you know what you are doing matters and that you matter as you do it—just because you are you. The way is your way—and now you're ready to connect your potential through it.

On the note of potential around us, as you read these words, something else is happening as well, a community, a movement of potential connectors is forming through the Connecting Potential Community Hub. Because you matter to me, I am excited to formally extend you an invitation to join what I intend to become a global movement. You can find the invitation here:

www.connectingpotential.ca

Little did that learner know all those years ago that she would be so bold as to extend such an invitation to you now! Potential did, and that is the power of connecting it. What are you waiting for? Let's continue connecting our potential together!

Whether you join us in the online community or create a connect potential movement in your world, in your way just by being you, know this—it's all connected. We're all connected. Influence anything, you influence everything. For that, and for you, I am grateful.

This is not the end, but the beginning, of your next adventure in connecting potential.

POTENTIAL

ONE Mindset Shift

**From *Problem* to *Potential*,
grounding in what matters**

ONE Operating System

ACT, FEEL, THINK

Disconnected Operating System =
Strain, Swirl, Stuck

- **Strain:** I can move, but it is hard and it hurts.
- **Swirl:** I can't stop but I am getting nowhere.
- **Stuck:** I can't move.

Connected Operating System =
Energy, Ease, Effectiveness

- **Energy:** I have energy to move; each move energizes me!
- **Ease:** I am relaxed and full of ease.
- **Effectiveness:** My actions lead to the outcomes I desire.

ONE Core Practice

INTEND, NOTICE, MOVE

Intend draws us forward.
Notice grounds us to take the first step.
The **creative tension** between the two gives us energy to move,
Move gets us from where we are to where we want to go.

THREE Dimensions of Exponential Impact

INTEND, NOTICE, MOVE

Within us as individuals
Between us in our relationships and teams
Around us in the cultures we co-create and contribute to

**REMEMBER THAT MATTERING MATTERS
AND YOU MATTER!**

**JOIN US FOR MORE ON THE
CONNECTING POTENTIAL COMMUNITY HUB**

www.connectingpotential.ca

BIBLIOGRAPHY

Cleveland Clinic. "Sympathetic Nervous System (SNS): What It Is & Function." June 6, 2022. https://my.clevelandclinic.org/health/body/23262-sympathetic-nervous-system-sns-fight-or-flight. Accessed October 17, 2023.

Cleveland Clinic. "Parasympathetic Nervous System (PSNS): What It Is & Function." https://my.clevelandclinic.org/health/body/23266-parasympathetic-nervous-system-psns#:~:text=A%20note%20from%20Cleveland%20Clinic&text=It%20helps%20relax%20you%20in. Accessed October 17, 2023.

Dennison, Paul. "Brain Gym." https://breakthroughsinternational.org/about/brain-gym/. Accessed October 17, 2023.

Dennison, Paul. "Brain Gym Bookstore." February 25, 2017. https://www.braingym.com/about/. Accessed October 17, 2023.

Fogel, Alan. "Emotional and Physical Pain Activate Similar Brain Regions." *Psychology Today.* April 19, 2012. https://www.psychologytoday.com/ca/blog/body-sense/201204/emotional-and-physical-pain-activate-similar-brain-regions. Accessed October 17, 2023.

Huberman, Andrew. "Huberman Lab." https://www.hubermanlab.com/. Accessed October 17, 2023.

Jensen, Peter. "Peter Jensen | Speaker / Author / Teacher / Ph.D in Sport Psychology." https://peterjensen.ca/. Accessed October 17, 2023.

Kotter, John P., and Dan S. Cohen. *The Heart of Change: Real-Life Stories of How People Change Their Organizations.* Boston, Mass: Harvard Business Review Press, 2012.

Medina, John. *Brain Rules (Updated and Expanded): 12 Principles for Surviving and Thriving at Work, Home, and School.* Seattle, WA: Pear Press, 2014.

Nosco, Stephanie. "Stephanie Nosco." https://stephanienosco.com/. Accessed October 17, 2023.

"Organization and Relationship Systems Coaching (ORSC)." CRR Global. https://crrglobal.com/about/orsc/. Accessed October 17, 2023.

Palmer, Parker J. *Let Your Life Speak: Listening for the Voice of Vocation.* San Francisco, Calif: Jossey-Bass, 1999.

Rock, Dr David, and Dr Al H. Ringleb. *Handbook of NeuroLeadership.* CreateSpace Independent Publishing Platform, 2013.

Schein, Edgar H. *Organizational Culture and Leadership.* Fourth edition. San Francisco, Calif: Jossey-Bass, 2010.

Scott, Susan. *Fierce Conversations: Achieving Success at Work and in Life One Conversation at a Time.* New York: Berkley, 2004.

Scott, Susan. *Fierce Leadership: A Bold Alternative to the Worst "Best" Practices of Business Today.* Crown Business, 2009.

Senge, Peter M. *The Fifth Discipline: The Art and Practice of the Learning Organization.* New York: Doubleday, 2006.

Siegel, Dan. "Hand Model of the Brain." https://drdansiegel.com/hand-model-of-the-brain/. Accessed October 17, 2023.

Sinek, Simon. *Start with Why: How Great Leaders Inspire Everyone to Take Action.* London: Portfolio/Penguin, 2009.

Stinson, Adrienne. "Box Breathing: How to Do It, Benefits, and Tips." Medical News Today. June 1, 2018. https://www.medicalnewstoday.com/articles/321805#:~:text=close%20their%20eyes%20and%20then. Accessed October 17, 2023.

Tamlyn, Rick. *The Weekly Yes, And Podcast.* "Episode 74: It's All Made up with Rick Tamlyn." Www.podbean.com. https://www.podbean.com/

premium-podcast/liveyesand/RXOV2wi3jC2m. Accessed October 17, 2023.

Watson, Stephanie. "Feel-Good Hormones: How They Affect Your Mind, Mood and Body." *Harvard Health.* July 20, 2021. https://www. health.harvard.edu/mind-and-mood/feel-good-hormones-how-they-affect-your-mind-mood-and-body#:~:text=What%20are%20the%20 four%20feel. Accessed October 17, 2023.

Weerd, Frank Uit de, and Marita Fridjhon. *Systems Inspired Leadership: How to Tap Collective Wisdom to Navigate Change, Enhance Agility, and Foster Collaboration.* CRR Global, 2021.

ACKNOWLEDGMENTS

Writing this book challenged me in ways that other learning has not. While I was the one to do the work, I am grateful that I did not have to do it alone. Deciding who to acknowledge formally is daunting because if I were to include everyone I want to, this section would need multiple volumes. So, if you are reading this and have been part of my learning journey and this book in any way, please know that **our connection and you made a difference.**

As a first-time author, I didn't know what I didn't know. This book would have never gone from potential to reality without the generous challenge and support of Ashley Mansour and her fantastic team at LA Writing Coach and Brands Through Books, including insightful writing coaches Jess and Melody, developmental editor Tayrn, organizational wizards Shelly and Chelsea, and publishing package copywriter Daisy. This team believed in the potential of *Potential,* and as a result, it became *matter.* There are not enough words to express my deep gratitude for Ashley, who not only led and expertly guided me through the process but developed me into an author, an identity I did not hold initially. Working with her was not only critical to connecting the potential of this book but also to me connecting mine as a professional and a person. **Without all of them, this book would not have been written**.

Speaking of not doing it alone, I want to acknowledge the Author Accelerator cohort who were with me and the book through its inception and completion. This diverse group of fiction and nonfiction authors cocreated a learning space where the potential that we connected between and around us also profoundly influenced the potential within me and this book (remember, that's how it works because we are all connected. Influence anything. Influence everything!). **Without them, you would have read a very different book.**

"I had coffee with my publisher in New York" became a statement I shared with many as I worked with Post Hill Press in the final editing, design, and bringing of *Potential* into the world. I followed this statement: "There's no story, I just like saying that." (insert smile emoji). Seriously, this statement shows my gratitude and amazement at being a published author. Anthony Ziccardi (my publisher) saw the potential in *Potential* as I began to believe in it, and his team took the book from a solid manuscript into an actual book! Right now, I am working closely with my associate publisher, Maddie, who led me through the rigid, minimal structure of completing *Potential* with a critical focus and an open mind. No question was too small, and throughout the process, Anthony and Maddie challenged and supported the production of a book that I am proud to offer the world and ownership of the identity *published author*, teaching me the ins, outs, and nuances of the publishing and book marketing world. To my line and proofing editor, Clayton, thank you for being the eyes I could not bring with your sharp attention to detail. And finally, to members of the Post Hill team I have not yet worked with, thank you for bringing *Potential* into the world! **Without them, this book would not be a tangible reality.**

I am fortunate to work with many wonderful clients and colleagues across Canada and beyond. Setting out on my Connecting Potential business journey, I was clear that my ideal clients were "purpose-driven, vision-led leaders, teams, and organizations who believe in the potential of their people for real and are willing to do the real work of connecting it." And because energy follows intention, those are the clients I work with. It was so hard to choose stories of just a few for this book, yet the ones I did share capture the courage and commitment it takes to connect potential that I experience working with all of my clients. Thank you to SAIT, WestJet, Rümi, Lavender, and Northland Properties (Denny's) for showing others what's possible when potential is connected. And thank you, Simon Sinek, for that conversation in a Brooklyn loft all those years ago, where I was first able to articulate the power of the potential around us. **Without**

them, the ideas shared in this book would only be interesting, not practical.

For me, the line between clients, colleagues, and friends is permeable because while the relationships have different aspects, they are still relationships at the core. Again, there are far too many relationships for me to acknowledge in the creation of this book, so for now, thanks to Michelle (leader in the "tough" conversation and all things leadership), Susan (counselor and Brain Gym inspiration), Stephanie (teacher and guide in deep mindfulness and embodiment work), and Jamey (fellow entrepreneur and nourisher of all things with love). The continual thread of our relationships was instrumental for *Potential* and me as its author. **Without them, this book would not be grounded in its relational voice.**

One other relationship not shared in this book that carried me through the journey of its writing must be acknowledged; perhaps it was too close and too sacred to describe to the world adequately. Thank you to my lifelong friend Shauna, whose courage and grace through her years-long cancer battle have both humbled and inspired me. You will never meet a person with greater resilience who does it, meeting each day, each challenge, each connection, as fully as she does. **Without her, this book would not feel as real.**

And my family. My brother Jeff, whose accomplishments are outshone by who he is. I am proud and grateful to be his big sister. My husband Don, whose unconditional love, challenge, and support made this book possible and my lifelong mental health journey one of healing and living a well and abundant life. There is no one who I have ever met or will ever encounter who brings out the best in me as he does in his steadfast, unwavering way. And for over the years, modeling for our sons what it is to be a man of integrity and commitment. Cayden and Jarrett—being the mother of these incredible young men has been my most significant gift and learning. Thank you for teaching me what it is to "be who you are" and uncompromising in this conviction despite what the world may attempt to trick us into believing and doing. (Thank you also to Chris Hadfield for putting to words the "impossible dream" that captures the essence of what both boys strive for.) **Without them, the voice of this book might not have been fully mine.**

Finally, to *potential* for turning a "small p" concept into the "big P" book of its title. I am not exactly sure when you took over and led me to what you wanted to be, and I am grateful you did. **Without you, there is no *Potential*.**

ABOUT THE AUTHOR

Pam August guides organizations, teams, and leaders to unlock the potential that is already there for transformational results. She was the director of culture activation at WestJet, one of Canada's most admired corporate cultures, where for fourteen years she was a fierce champion and developer of people and culture as a key enabler of strategic success. Today, she is a trusted partner for high-performance organizations around the world through her firm, Connecting Potential. With deep and diverse experience, she knows what it takes to uncover, align, and activate the best of what organizations already offer and what they can develop into. Pam is a sought-after speaker, facilitator, coach, and cocreator with a strong foundation of lifelong learning. She has a Bachelor of Adult Education, a Master of Arts in Leadership, and is certified as an Organization and Relationships Systems (ORSC) and brain-based coach. Pam takes pleasure in solving tricky problems, listening deeply, learning always, and laughing—a lot.